"Deserves a spot on the bookshelf of every biotech CFO."

—*Bruce Booth, Partner, Atlas Venture*

"Drug development is exceedingly difficult and fraught with scientific risk. Building financial models to accurately forecast the revenue potential, expense, and valuation of drugs in clinical development is only slightly less challenging. *The Pharmagellan Guide to Biotech Forecasting and Valuation* by Frank David and colleagues is a helpful and insightful resource for anyone who finds themselves staring at a blank Excel spreadsheet."

—*Adam Feuerstein, Senior Columnist, TheStreet.com*

"Frank and his colleagues have written a fantastic plain-English guide to building a valuation model for a biotech product or portfolio. It manages to be both conversational and rigorous, citing primary data supporting the assumptions made throughout—and encourages you to do the same. And it's unceasingly pragmatic—it encourages you to eschew precision in favor of accuracy. Some issues are simply unknowable today or too small to matter in the grand scheme of things, so why obsess over them? If you're trying to develop a reasonable view of the value of your program or your company—and a view that will appear reasonable to the folks across the table—whether it's to support a financing, a licensing transaction, an acquisition, or just dreaming about what your company will be worth some day—this beautiful book breaks it down for you."

—*Michael Gilman, Advisor, Atlas Venture;*
serial biotech CEO (Stromedix, Padlock Therapeutics)

"An invaluable, rigorously detailed, and well-validated guide to assessing drug development programs and opportunities—certain to raise biotech analysts' confidence in their models and forecasts."

—*John Sullivan, Director of Equity Research and Healthcare Investment Strategist,*
Leerink Partners

"Pragmatic, credible advice on financial modeling for biotech executives. This is the book I wish I'd had when I started out in the industry—it would have saved me hours of time."

—*Vin Milano, CEO, Idera Pharmaceuticals*

"To be a successful investor in biotechnology requires a grasp of medicine, familiarity with a company's management team, and the ability to translate that knowledge into complex quantitative models. Price and value are often two very different things, so you need to always have your own opinion about the latter precisely modeled. *The Pharmagellan Guide to Biotech Forecasting and Valuation* does an excellent job of defining the inputs that go into modeling, explains how they can be forecasted, and shows how it all ties together. I'd recommend it to anyone looking to better understand one of the most difficult sides of this business."

—*Brad Loncar, CEO, Loncar Investments*

"Clear, well-written, and very useful in our mission to better serve our patients."

—*Jim Geraghty, Chairman of the Board of Directors, Idera Pharmaceuticals*

"This book offers a great explanation of the inputs and assumptions for biotech models, and how to think about them. I highly recommend it, both to people who build the models and people like me who have to look at them."

—*Briggs Morrison, CEO, Syndax Pharmaceuticals*

THE PHARMAGELLAN GUIDE TO BIOTECH FORECASTING AND VALUATION

Frank S. David
Seth Robey
Andrew Matthews

Requests for permission should be addressed to: info@pharmagellan.com.

This book may be purchased for educational, business, or sales promotional use. For information, please visit www.pharmagellan.com.

First edition

Edited by Robert Simison

Designed by Denise Clifton

ISBN-13: 978-0-9984075-0-0

10 9 8 7 6 5 4 3 2 1

Printed in the United States of America

CONTENTS

FOREWORD

WHEN IS A BIOTECHNOLOGY COMPANY truly viable, and when is it a meandering science project?

As a life sciences portfolio manager, I ask that question first when evaluating a potential new investment, and as a college instructor teaching entrepreneurship to science and engineering students, I try to prepare my students to be ready with a convincing answer.

For both students and experienced management teams, this is no small task. With revenue and profit years in the future, and a multistep development process fraught with uncertainty in between, early-stage biotech companies are a challenge to model. Their viability is difficult to handicap. Successful companies need to construct a credible narrative that connects today's uncertainty with the pathway to future success.

That narrative needs believable financial models.

With product development times exceeding 10 years, biotech is unique among economic sectors. Every path to success is littered with clinical and regulatory obstacles, and each of them has the potential to bring development to a crashing halt. It's hard to define straightforward means and deviations for simple variables like product penetration and pricing years in advance. And predicting capital-market dynamics relative to the company's periodic needs for capital is close to guesswork. Every early-stage biotech is one market downturn–delayed secondary offering away from needing a recapitalization. And such an event would invalidate any prior decision making.

These factors make it easy to dismiss biotechnology forecasting, modeling, and valuation as mere guesswork, support for wishful thinking, or a method for reverse-engineering whatever arbitrary outcome the modeler wants to justify.

With this volume, however, Frank S. David, Seth Robey, and Andrew Matthews demonstrate the power of biotech forecasting and valuation. They have produced a best-practices manual that makes poor decisions based on incorrect assumptions less likely for biotech entrepreneurs or investors. They are also less likely to do the wrong things for the wrong reasons.

Business financial modeling exists on a continuum starting with the defined, predictive, and quite accurate discounted cash flow equations of fixed income and credit analysis. It then passes though the open-ended but still narrow-ranged stock dividend models appropriate for mature industries and steady cash flow–generating profitable companies. It ultimately ends with the metric-starved, pre-revenue biotechnology discovery and development companies.

Financial modeling has been serially abused by sell-side equity analysts to derive short-term "price targets," decoupled by second-decimal-point precision from the best-guess aspect of underlying assumptions. Given this degree of uncertainty, why participate at all in an exercise that mistakes precision for accuracy?

Because to not do so is worse. We model our financial predictions for the same reasons we write business plans: to explicitly define our assumptions, formalize our logic and decision making, and provide a basic road map. We can thoughtfully deviate from the map as we make the transition from imagination to reality and from abstract idea to tangible benefit for customer, client, or patient. To model is to tether ourselves to future expectations grounded in today's best realities. Modeling gives our investors, collaborators, partners, and future customers a means by which to judge our progress and critique our thinking.

The authors build a comprehensive scaffold for collecting present facts to support credible expectations. Incidence and prevalence data, real-world adherence and compliance statistics, pricing models based on both history and current trend, commercialization data and exclusivity are all built into revenue models. Industry benchmarks, industry data sets, and the authors' own research-based assumptions for multipliers, growth, and discount rates are translated into expense and then valuation models.

The authors clearly label discretionary variables, such as a 2% annual assumption for price increases in early-stage forecasts. They clearly state and support the rationale for specific numbers. The result is a rational and logical guide to biotechnology forecasting, a worthy and needed resource for a process that—done correctly—replaces guesswork and uncertainty with precision and clarity.

David Sable, MD
Portfolio Manager, Special Situations Life Sciences Fund
Lecturer, Department of Biological Sciences Biotechnology Program,
Columbia University

1

PREPARING TO BUILD A BIOTECH FINANCIAL MODEL

All models are wrong, but some are useful. —G. E. P. Box[1]

FINANCIAL FORECASTS and valuation models of R&D-stage drug candidates are almost always wrong—and sometimes wildly so.[2] The inputs have error bars a mile wide. But by selecting specific numbers to plug into an Excel spreadsheet, we do ourselves a double disservice. We almost certainly guarantee we'll be wrong. And we give ourselves and others a false sense of accuracy in the face of the inherently dynamic and unpredictable nature of drug R&D and commercialization.[3,4]

So why do we build biotech financial models? From an intellectual point of view, they force us to put a stake in the ground on key assumptions, and they can help us figure out which levers we can pull to increase profits or value. They also help to define the areas of key uncertainty and risk, and force us to wrestle with how comfortable we are with the drivers that are beyond our control.[5]

But there's also a practical reason: often, we just have to.

- Many management teams, boards, R&D leaders, and portfolio managers in biotech and pharma use forecasts and net present value (NPV) calculations to help decide how to allocate scarce resources toward early-stage projects.
- In acquisition and licensing discussions, business development professionals and investment bankers on both sides of the table build models

to assess the attractiveness of the deal and, particularly in pharma, get approval to make the purchase.

- Many biotech investors routinely build models to assess the likely performance of public or private investments (although venture capitalists often eschew them in favor of valuations based on comparable deals and expected exits).[6]

The problem, of course, is that although the consumers of financial models of pre-commercial drugs—executives, bosses, investors, board members, and other stakeholders—know that they are inherently imprecise, they still want the inputs to be logical and data-driven. So even though a drug's market launch may be close to a decade in the future, you may be asked how you reached your estimate of the size and cost of the sales force that will be needed to support it.

If this scenario sounds wildly implausible, wholly uninteresting, or both, stop reading. But if you've ever had the desire or need to build a biotech model that is as well vetted and thoughtful as possible given the level of uncertainty inherent in the enterprise, then this book is meant for you.

How to use this book—and how *not* to

This book is intended to provide citable, vetted references for many key inputs in financial models of early-stage drug candidates—and in particular to develop and justify reasonable estimates for key components when a high degree of precision is simply impossible.

We've written this as a quick-reference handbook, so you can flip to a key section, read about the particular aspect that interests you, and continue on your merry way. The sections are organized into the three general categories of issues we encounter when we build biotech financial models: those related to income forecasting, expense forecasting, and valuation.

Throughout this book, we've sought to present data and references that you can use as justification for your modeling choices, or as a jumping-off point to creating your own inputs. The data come primarily from journal articles, white papers, and other publications, and our own proprietary analyses. With regard to the last category, we've tried to provide as much transparency as possible regarding our methodology so that you can repeat or extend our analyses as desired.

Importantly, we have made three major assumptions about you, our reader, which we hope you will consider carefully as you use this book:

- We assume you **already know how to build and analyze a basic financial forecast and discounted cash flow model.** This book is not a textbook. Basic financial modeling and analysis are covered in many corporate finance textbooks and some excellent online resources.[7] There are also some biopharma-specific introductions that you might find helpful.[8,9,10]

- We also assume you **need approximate inputs to incorporate into your model.** This book is not a substitute for granular, specific detail on individual drugs, companies, or markets, particularly when an asset is nearly launched or already commercialized. If you have hard numbers on your own company's G&A expenses, or primary market research data on projected uptake of your drug, then please use them. This book is specifically intended to guide you in "data-free" zones—and is therefore most applicable to drug programs and companies in early- to mid-stages of clinical development.

- Finally, we assume you **know the basics of patient-driven forecasting in biopharma.** Although we have included a chapter addressing some key questions and issues in estimating the size of your addressable patient population, for more depth on this topic we refer you to other sources of general[11] and biopharma-specific[12,13] information.

How to cite and use the information in this book

All material in this book is copyrighted. For information on licensing portions for purposes that fall outside "fair use," please contact us at info@pharmagellan.com.

Looking ahead

We call this the "first edition" intentionally—it's a living document, with plenty of room for improvement and expansion. If you see something we missed or got wrong, please drop us a line at info@pharmagellan.com. You'll earn our heartfelt thanks, and we'll acknowledge you in the next edition if we incorporate your feedback.

INCOME

2

ADDRESSABLE PATIENT POPULATION

MOST STRATEGY and business development discussions require a "bottoms-up," patient-driven model, using the number of addressable patients to estimate the market opportunity. This approach transparently shows the logic of how the patient population was identified and allows one to independently model the disease epidemiology separately from other factors such as dosing, compliance, and pricing.

The standard flow through a patient-driven biotech financial model addresses three main questions:

1. How many patients are there?
2. How are they subdivided—and which subset(s) are we aiming to treat?
3. How many of them will get diagnosed and treated?

Rather than attempting to comprehensively address every possible scenario for defining the total addressable patient population, in this chapter we'll focus on a few common situations and challenges. For more general guidance, please consult other resources on market segmentation and sizing specific to drug forecasting[14,15] or applicable more generally across industries.[16]

Incidence and prevalence

Epidemiologic data are typically reported as incidence or prevalence, and depending on the clinical situation, one or the other will typically be more relevant to your model.[17] For example:

- Many acute-care therapies are "one and done"—for example, treatments related to acute infections, postoperative pain, or acute stroke management. Each incident patient will get a single treatment or course of therapy that resolves the illness, leaving no prevalent population.
- For many chronic diseases, such as asthma, diabetes, hypertension, and schizophrenia, patients are treated for all or most of their lives after diagnosis. In these cases, the maximum opportunity is typically measured as the size of the prevalent population.

Although these examples make it seem that incidence is more relevant to acute illnesses and prevalence to chronic ones, this is not always the case. It's crucial to have a detailed clinical understanding of the patient population your therapy seeks to address in order to use the right epidemiologic data. For example:

- Anticoagulants for secondary prevention of stroke are taken chronically, but the population size is defined by the incidence of strokes.
- Many onetime (acute) interventions can be used in a prevalent (chronic illness) population—for example, gastric bypass for obesity.

Once you decide incidence or prevalence is more relevant to your model, you need to obtain data from government health agencies, the peer-reviewed medical literature, or other reputable sources. We commonly see three pitfalls when forecasters incorporate these data into financial projections:

1. **Incomplete understanding of epidemiologic methods:** It is crucial to understand whether the numbers reported in an epidemiologic study reflect underlying incidence or prevalence (e.g., in an unselected population), or if they already take diagnosis and/or treatment rates into account (e.g., in a population that has already come to medical attention).
2. **Use of poor-quality data:** In rare diseases, it is often challenging to obtain multiple well-conducted studies from which to confirm epidemiologic data. In these cases, it may make sense to calculate revenues and valuations under a range of scenarios, rather than arbitrarily committing to a single population size.

3. **Reliance on studies with nonrepresentative demographics:** The addressable population for a disease may depend on underlying differences in race, socioeconomics, or other factors that may not be reflected in the group studied in published analyses. This problem is particularly common when one extrapolates U.S. epidemiology from studies conducted in small regions of Europe.

Side note—Interconverting incidence and prevalence: Occasionally, you will be able to obtain either incidence or prevalence data for a given clinical entity—but not both—and will need the other to build your model. To do this, you can use the fact that the prevalence (cases per population) is the product of the incidence (cases per person per year) and the number of years a patient lives with a disease after diagnosis (until death or disease resolution).[18,19] In other words:

$$Incidence = \frac{Prevalence}{Disease\ duration}$$

Subdividing the patient population

In most diseases, only some patients are eligible or appropriate for a given therapy. This subdivision is usually made on clinical or pathological grounds and varies substantially by disease or indication. From a modeling standpoint, it's important to ensure that the subdivision method you're using is in line with how physicians make treatment decisions. Some of the most common segmentation approaches are based on:

- Anatomic stage (e.g., regionally advanced vs. metastatic cancer).
- Contraindications (e.g., clinical comorbidities, other medications).
- Demographics (e.g., pediatric vs. adult).
- Disease severity (e.g., mild/moderate/severe psoriasis; NYHA classes for heart failure).
- Pathology/lab results.

There are data to inform how to account for many well-established disease subdivisions in financial models. But for other subdivisions—particularly more qualitative "mild/moderate/severe" classifications—it can often be helpful to obtain expert input or data from a small market research study to give more credibility to the inputs.

Diagnosis rates

It's extremely important to account for diagnosis rates when converting epidemiologic data into an addressable population. Consider the following examples:

- For generally asymptomatic diseases like hyperlipidemia or osteoporosis, the size of the addressable population for primary prevention depends on the use (and reimbursement) of screening tests in healthy people.
- For illnesses diagnosed late in the pathologic course, like Alzheimer's disease, the opportunity to treat early-stage patients with disease-modifying agents may be limited by the availability and use of screening tests.[20]
- The effective prevalence of diseases with evolving clinical definitions, like overactive bladder, depends on how awareness increases and diagnostic standards evolve.[21]

From a global perspective, it should go without saying that the underlying dynamics of disease diagnosis can vary greatly between countries depending on practice norms, technology access, and the regulatory and reimbursement status of diagnostic tests. This is particularly true for certain types of imaging and molecular diagnostic tests that may be less available outside the United States.

Treatment rates

Just because a patient has been diagnosed with a disease does not mean he or she is appropriate for drug therapy. Here are examples of cases in which a treatment rate far lower than 100% should be incorporated into a financial model:

Illnesses with significant nonmedical therapies: In diseases like obesity and depression, which have several classes of therapeutic options, the addressable market may be only those patients who have been deemed appropriate for medical therapy, as opposed to lifestyle changes, surgical/device-based interventions, or other nondrug therapies.

Mild-disease subsets: Depending on the severity of the illness, its consequences, and the relative burden of treatment (including side effects, exposure to potential harms, and "hassle"), a significant fraction of lightly afflicted patients may opt against receiving any drug therapy.

Early disease with low conversion rates: In several types of cancer, there are ongoing debates about whether some patients with early-stage lesions detected by screening tests may be "overdiagnosed" and poor candidates for therapy.[22]

Diseases with evolving standards of care: As mentioned above in the context of diagnostics, there may be no clear consensus on whether or how to treat patients diagnosed with "new" diseases like overactive bladder whose definitions, clinical courses, and pathologies are still being defined.

3

ADHERENCE AND COMPLIANCE

IN THEORY, EVERY PATIENT will fill every prescription and take every prescribed dose of a drug. But in reality, this is not the case.[23] For acute-care outpatient therapies, some patients don't fill even the first prescription. For chronic-care outpatient therapies, some patients don't fill the prescriptions on time if at all (and thus miss days of therapy), and of those who do, some don't take all of the doses as directed (and thus obtain fewer refills over the course of a year).

Many early-stage biotechs choose to ignore any factor in financial models that could reduce the maximum projected revenue. However, including a data-driven estimate for adherence/compliance reflects a more sophisticated appreciation of the real-world dynamics of prescription drug sales. This also helps avoid overexuberant revenue projections and builds credibility with internal stakeholders and potential financial and strategic partners.

Framework for accounting for adherence/compliance

In a biotech financial model, there are three main reasons why the sales of a drug may be less than what's expected based on the number of prescribed doses:

1. Patient does not fill the initial prescription.
2. Patient does not fill the refill(s).
3. Patient skips doses (either accidentally or on purpose) and as a result obtains refills les frequently than expected.

These phenomena are variously known as "adherence," "compliance," "persistence," and "concordance."[24] Wide variability in terminology and methods makes it hard to assess published papers and determine accurate values for a revenue model.

For drugs that are on or near the market, it's critically important to understand in great detail how patients are likely to fill prescriptions—but for early-stage biotechs, this is typically overkill. In most financial models of R&D-stage drugs, we find it's easiest and clearest to use a single, aggregate factor to account for "adherence/compliance"—provided we are armed with the appropriate rationale and references.

In the case of drugs administered in physicians' offices or inpatient settings, adherence/compliance is less of an issue. So in this chapter, as in our practice, we will consider the problem mainly in relation to patient-administered ambulatory care agents.

Adherence/compliance in various settings

Acute care outpatient adherence/compliance

For outpatient prescriptions that will be filled only once (e.g., acute antibiotics), the most relevant research for financial modeling measures **"primary adherence"**—or how often the first prescription is filled.

Once the patient fills the prescription, we're less concerned with how many doses are actually taken—but these data are often a component in published adherence studies. So using values from these more-general adherence studies will typically cause you to underestimate revenue.

We generally assume an adherence/compliance rate of about 85% for acute care outpatient medicines. At the high end, one analysis of almost 600,000 prescriptions for anti-infectives in a U.S. managed-care setting showed more than 97% primary adherence.[25] But a separate study of almost 40,000 prescriptions to Canadian patients for bronchitis and urinary tract infections found primary adherence rates of just 79%.[26] For building financial models, we find that even in the most compelling clinical cases, ambulatory adherence/compliance estimates above 90% are not typically credible, regardless of the apparent strength of supporting data.

Chronic care outpatient adherence/compliance

For chronic therapies, the data on adherence/compliance that most logically apply to financial models measure the **"medication possession ratio," or MPR**.[27] The MPR takes the number of doses in a patient's possession in a year and divides it by the number that should have been consumed in a year. Thus, the MPR goes down when patients obtain fewer than the expected number of refills in a year, or when they "stretch" a prescription by taking the prescribed number of doses over more days.

We typically assume a base adherence/compliance rate of around 70% in chronic ambulatory care. That is in line with rates for the most frequently prescribed drugs in a large European observational cohort across multiple indications.[28,29] However, this estimate masks the wide variability of MPR values reported for different drugs, drug classes, and indications in outpatient chronic care. This makes it challenging to define comparators for a financial model.

Factors influencing adherence/compliance

For the vast majority of early-stage assets, we do not attempt to customize the projected adherence/compliance rate in a financial model based on the drug's particular features (efficacy, dosing, safety, tolerability, etc.) relative to those of competitors. Instead, we make a middle-of-the-road assumption to avoid adding complexity and a false sense of precision. This approach is straightforward, intuitive, and defensible, particularly for assets in Phase 2 or earlier.

But in cases when improved adherence/compliance is absolutely central to the drug's value proposition, we consider making adjustments based on various factors, including:

Disease symptoms: MPR is generally lower (50%–70%) for asymptomatic diseases like hyperlipidemia and hypertension.[30,31] And in some symptomatic illnesses like gastroesophageal reflux disease, a majority of patients may self-titrate dosing based on their symptoms, leading to a lower MPR.[32]

Disease severity and perceived medication effectiveness: Some of the highest reported MPRs in the literature—well over 80% in some cases—have been in diseases like chronic myelogenous leukemia and multiple sclerosis.[33,34,35,36]

Dosing frequency: Not unexpectedly, MPR increases as dose frequency decreases from multiple times a day to daily to weekly.[37,38,39,40]

Polypharmacy: Several studies have demonstrated that MPR is higher for fixed-dose combinations than for separate medicines, and adherence falls as patients take additional drugs.[41,42,43,44]

"Special cases": It is always worth conducting a literature review to determine whether a particular indication is a significant outlier on adherence/compliance, or whether the data are inconsistent. For example, MPR data for chronic pain medications are particularly variable, with reported values ranging from the low teens to more than 80%.[45,46,47,48,49,50] And in bipolar disorder, almost all reported MPR values are below 50%.[51,52,53,54]

4

PRICING

PRICING IS ONE OF THE LARGEST UNKNOWNS and one of the most significant revenue drivers in financial forecasts for early-stage biotechs. As a result, the most credible approach in most situations is to be transparent, logical, and conservative when modeling drug prices.

When a drug is close to or on the market, it makes sense to robustly characterize the current or projected market access, rebates, discounts, et cetera, through secondary data analyses and primary research with payers and other pricing stakeholders. But at earlier stages of R&D, in the absence of detailed pricing information, the most appropriate approach is to:

- Model a U.S. starting price as if the drug were on the market today, based on comparisons to appropriate treatments.
- Incorporate modest annual increases (typically in line with inflation) to calculate the price at launch and thereafter.
- Model prices in other countries and regions by applying a correction factor to the U.S. price at launch, and apply a country- or region-specific annual rate of increase.

Before we begin—an in-the-weeds note on dosing: It's critical in biotech models to translate the per-dose price into projected annual revenue per patient. For example, according to Medicare Part B data,[55] Avastin (bevacizumab) was priced at about $70 per 10 mg in late 2015. However, Avastin is dosed at 5–10 mg/kg every two weeks,[56] so the actual monthly cost (to the end user) per patient (assuming a typical 80 kg American)[57] is $5,600–$11,200—and the yearly cost will depend on the number of months of therapy projected for a given indication. We recommend adding extra rows to your spreadsheet to convert per-dose price data into projected revenue per patient per year to transparently anchor the model to comparator data obtained from secondary research.

Key U.S. pricing definitions

It's important to understand some basic terms that are used in U.S. pricing.[58,59] From lowest to highest dollar amounts, the four key numbers are:

1. **ASP (average sales price)**—Price paid to manufacturers, net of all rebates and discounts. *This is the number you want to incorporate into your model.*
2. **WAC (wholesale acquisition cost)**—"List price" paid by the wholesaler to the manufacturer, before rebates and discounts.
3. **Retail price**—Price charged by the distributor to the end user.
4. **AWP (average wholesale price)**—Manufacturer-reported "sticker price," which is a premium to WAC.

The difference between ASP and WAC reflects the wholesaler's margin, including discounts and rebates offered by the manufacturer. The difference between WAC and retail reflects the retailer's margin.

You'll find comparator price data in various formats. Here are general rules for how to convert them:

TABLE 4-1: Relationships between key pricing variables.

	Referenced to AWP=100	Referenced to Retail=100	Referenced to WAC=100	Referenced to ASP=100
AWP	100	107	120	135
Retail	93	100	112	126
WAC	84	90	100	113
ASP	74	79	88	100

Benchmark multiples to interconvert between AWP (average wholesale price), retail price, WAC (wholesale acquisition cost), and ASP (average sales price).

These conversion factors are based on the following inputs:

- A 2005 analysis of more than 700 single-source branded drugs that found median ASP was 74% of AWP.[60]
- Since a federal legal settlement in 2009, AWP has been capped at 120% of WAC.[61]
- Retail pharmacy margins over WAC on branded prescription drugs are typically 5%–15%.[62]

Importantly, in drug categories with intense payer pressure (especially primary care markets with multiple competitors), there is often more significant discounting by manufacturers. There are also substantial discounts on outpatient medications provided to 340B providers that provide care to large numbers of underserved patients.[63] In these cases, it may be reasonable to further discount ASP relative to other pricing measures.

Comparator pricing data

We typically anchor the U.S. price on a reasonable comparator, based on the therapeutic area, mode of action, and other factors. Regardless of whether the comparator is a single agent or the average price of a group of similar drugs, we transparently report our methodology and sources to demonstrate our thought process and rationale.

Although it can be challenging to obtain reliable price data, there are a few general resources and approaches:

ASP: These data are freely available only for a subset of physician-administered drugs covered under Medicare Part B.[64]

AWP, WAC: The Federal NADAC (National Average Drug Acquisition Cost) database provides invoiced amounts paid by retail pharmacies to acquire drugs.[65] The NADAC prices are very closely comparable to WAC for single-source, branded pharmaceuticals.[66] In addition, paid sources of AWP and WAC data include PriceRx/Medi-Span[67] and the MicroMedex "Red Book"[68] (AWP only).

Retail: For outpatient medications, you can usually obtain updated retail prices from pharmacy chains like OptumRx, Walmart, or Walgreens. These data are more current than those in a 2012 survey conducted by the Centers for Medicare & Medicaid Services.[69]

Sometimes there are price data in reports from journalists, equity analysts, consultants, government agencies, et cetera, as well as companies' earnings calls and press releases. In these cases, it's critical to understand the context (and reliability of the source) to decide whether the price adequately corresponds to ASP, retail, or some other metric.

It is tempting to model a price premium for a new drug that will supposedly offer a significant improvement in care. In fact, most companies launch products at a higher price than that of competitors. However, we advocate anchoring a drug's price directly on that of one or more comparators. In our experience, most consumers of biotech financial forecasts see aggressive pricing as a red flag that impugns the model's credibility.

Annual price increases

We typically model a 2% annual price increase in early-stage forecasts. This is in line with general inflation and with a current estimate of U.S. net price increases on branded drugs published by QuintilesIMS.[70] This value and the underlying rationale resonate well with biotechs, investors, and potential strategic partners.

Based on historical benchmarks, one could theoretically justify projecting higher annual price increases of 10% or more—far in excess of inflation. Examples of studies that have quantified price increases higher than the rate of inflation include:

- An analysis of prices of 50 drugs from 2008 to 2014 across six categories (ADHD, asthma, oral diabetes, injectable diabetes, MS, and RA) found average compound annual growth rates (CAGRs) of 9% to 16%.[71]
- An AARP analysis of retail prices of 227 branded drugs "commonly used by older Americans" found that annual increases had climbed steadily over time, from 5.7% in 2006 to 12.9% in 2013.[72]

- Our analysis of a *Wall Street Journal* study of 30 top-selling drugs from 2010 to 2014 found an average CAGR of 15%, with a range of 6% to 28%.[73]

However, we do not recommend this strategy. Although aggressive price hikes are common in the industry, they are facing increasing public, media, and lawmaker attention in the current political climate.[74] Thus, building significant annual price increases into a model to inflate peak revenue and net present value estimates is ill-advised for most discussions with management, boards, investors, or potential strategic partners.

Global pricing considerations

To develop a patient-driven model for ex-U.S. regions, you need to incorporate relevant starting prices and increases, similar to the approach described above. In most major markets outside the United States, drug prices are substantially lower than in the American market because they are regulated by health economic calculations and external referencing (which excludes the States). We typically either use normalization factors for key markets to adjust U.S. ASP, or obtain direct price comparators from ex-U.S. markets.

Notably, although the analysis below is generally well suited for drugs that are relatively far from commercialization, it is somewhat oversimplified for those that are near to market. In reality, biopharma product teams tightly script the order of ex-U.S. launches based on how different countries reference one another's pricing of new agents.[75,76] But for drugs in mid-R&D, this level of nuance is generally not appropriate to incorporate into a forecast or valuation model.

Price as a function of U.S. ASP: In Europe and Japan—two ex-U.S. regions that are strategically and economically most important to most drugmakers, and typically included in product forecasts—we generally model prices of approximately 50% of those in the United States, based on cross-border comparison data.

Published studies comparing drug prices among countries use widely variable methods—including baskets of comparators, inclusion of generics, correction for currency exchange rates, year of analysis, and countries included.

Because all of the most relevant analyses include the United Kingdom, we adjusted each available data set to use the United Kingdom as the reference market with a value of 1. (See table below.) Then, we calculated the median price in each country (relative to the U.K.) across all of these studies. Finally, we readjusted these median values to use the United States as the reference market to allow for incorporation into biotech forecasts. Our full data set and analysis are shown below:

TABLE 4-2: International drug prices as a function of U.S. ASP.

	DE	ES	FR	IT	JP	UK	US
IMS Consulting (2003)[a,b]	1.03		0.90	0.95		1.00	1.61
U.S. Commerce Dept. (2004)[a]	1.11		1.04		0.70	1.00	2.13
PMPRB (2006a)[a]	1.01		0.88	0.79		1.00	1.62
Santésuisse (2006)[a]	1.01		0.85	0.80		1.00	
Office of Fair Trading (2007)[a]	1.08	0.84	0.96	0.84		1.00	1.98
Danzon (2008)[a]	0.97	0.82	0.84	0.76	1.06	1.00	1.32
U.K. OHE (2011)[77]	1.48	0.98	1.01	0.98		1.00	3.13
EvaluatePharma (2015)[78]	1.33		1.61		1.01	1.00	3.03
Median—normalized to the United Kingdom	1.06	0.84	0.93	0.82	1.01	1.00	1.98
Median—normalized to the United States	**0.53**	**0.42**	**0.47**	**0.41**	**0.51**	**0.51**	**1.00**

Benchmark multiples to allow interconversion between drug prices across the United States, Japan, and the EU-5. DE = Germany; ES = Spain; FR = France; IT = Italy; JP = Japan; UK = United Kingdom; US = United States. [a]Data extracted from references cited in report from Organisation for Economic Co-operation and Development (OECD).[79,b] Mean of values obtained using two different monetary conversion approaches.

Ex-U.S. price comparators for individual drugs: The following public resources for ex-U.S. drug prices can be helpful in some instances:

- Health Action International, a nongovernmental organization focused on pharmaceutical access, maintains a list of websites that provide national drug prices across a broad range of countries.[80]

- ZenRx provides price data across drugs and countries, but much of the data has not been updated since 2009–2013.[81]

Importantly, many data sources report retail prices of individual drugs, which are higher than ASP.[82] Thus, without additional country- or drug-specific data on retail-to-manufacturer discounts, it may be challenging to incorporate these data into a biotech financial model.

Rest of Europe / rest of world considerations: In general, most experts view the United States as an outlier for drug pricing. So for models of other European countries or the rest of the world, we typically assume pricing similar to the EU-5 countries as above.

Ex-U.S. yearly price changes: For most of the world outside the United States, including all of Europe, we generally assume either flat or slightly negative year-over-year price changes in biotech revenue models, based on existing policies and forecasted trends, including:

- A voluntary agreement between the British government and drugmakers capped the growth rate of pharmaceutical spending in the United Kingdom at 0% for 2014, rising to 1.9% in 2018.[83]
- Germany typically extracts price discounts once a drug's revenues reach approximately 250M euros, which would lead to net price declines.[84]
- In Japan, mandated price adjustments every two years have led to average annual price *decreases* of 2.8%, based on data showing a median price reduction of 15.5% from 2008 to 2014 across small molecules and biologics.[85]

5

MARKET SHARE

MOST BIOTECH FINANCIAL MODELS calculate the "total addressable market" (TAM)—or the total revenue potential of the entire segment that their product would target. Then they estimate the share that a new drug will capture, based mainly on the number of pre-existing competitors.

Estimating market share based on order of entry is typically an overly conservative case that assumes the new drug is only minimally differentiated from competitors. But that approach does serve as a useful anchor at the low end of the range of possibilities. At the same time, the TAM calculation provides the most extreme upside scenario of capturing the entire market and driving current drugs out of business.

When we build biotech financial models, we typically focus on defining these two extremes as credibly as possible. That's the focus of the first two sections of this chapter. At the end, we'll discuss the challenges of adjusting the expected share based on drug-specific factors.

Defining TAM and competitors

TAM: To calculate peak market share, one first needs to define the market, which requires some thought and planning. Imagine you're developing an oral medicine with a novel mechanism to treat a subset of diabetes patients. If you define the competitor set as all diabetes drugs—or maybe even all diabetes approaches, including diet and exercise—then you may have a huge TAM, but there will be many competitors and you will have a relatively small share. Alternatively, if you define the market as only the subset of patients specifically targeted by your drug who have failed to respond optimally to other therapies, the TAM will be smaller, but you may be the first (or only) entrant and capture most or all of the market. (See chapter 2 for more details.)

Competitors: Though it's usually straightforward to identify marketed competitors, it can be a challenge to account for development-stage products that have not yet launched—and may never do so. One could develop a probability-based model to account for all possible launch outcomes of these drugs, but this approach is overkill for most biotechs. In practice, we typically take one of the following approaches:

- When R&D-stage competitors are very early or perceived as high-risk, we typically ignore them and transparently stipulate so in our methodology.
- We occasionally include selected late-stage competitors in our model if we and other experts think they are highly likely to launch and disrupt the market.
- If there are a large number of early-stage products under development, we sometimes model an "amalgamated" competitor to reflect our assumption that one of these drugs will reach the market before we do, although we don't know which one.

Order of entry

Across most industries, it is generally accepted that there is a "first-mover advantage" with regard to market share—but what is the quantitative relationship between share and order of entry, particularly for prescription drugs?

Analyses from the 1980s and 1990s of consumer packaged goods and anti-ulcer prescription drugs suggest the following relationship:

$$MS_x = MS_1 * (\frac{1}{\sqrt{x}})$$

In this equation, X is the order of entry, MSx is the share of the xth entrant, and MS1 is the share of the first entrant.[86] By this math, the first entrant will retain about 58% of a two-player market and about 31% of a five-drug market.

Although this is a reasonable starting point, for biopharma models we adjust the output from this equation slightly to account for results from published analyses specific to the drug industry:

TABLE 5-1: Projected market share based on order of entry.

			Share for:		
	First drug	Second drug	Third drug	Fourth drug	Fifth drug
Two-drug market	60%	40%			
Three-drug market	40%	30%	30%		
Four-drug market	31%	23%	23%	23%	
Five-drug market	24%	19%	19%	19%	19%

Pharmagellan analysis based on reconciliation of published studies; see text for details.

Our assumptions are based on the following data:

- A recent analysis examined 492 drug launches across 131 medication classes from 1986 through 2012.[87] Comparing each drug's observed share to its "fair share" (1/n in an n-drug market), the authors found that the first entrant's boost was 11 percentage points in a two-drug market (61% vs. the expected 50%), but only 4 points when there are more than two entrants. The average bump was 6 percentage points across all markets. Further, in contrast with earlier findings in consumer packaged goods and antiulcer markets, these researchers found that the difference in share among the second through the fifth entrants was minimal. The main advantage went to the first-to-market drug.

- A 2015 study built an econometric model from sales and promotional spending data on 50 second-, third-, or fourth-to-market drugs approved by the FDA from 1988 to 2009.[88] The authors focused on agents that were minimally differentiated from the originator, as defined by lack of priority regulatory review by the FDA and their classification by France's Haute Autorité de Santé.[89] As might be predicted, these authors found a significant dependence on order of entry, promotional spending, and the time delay from launch of the previous entrant. The projected shares they found for these "me-too" agents were similar to those in the earlier work on consumer packaged goods and antiulcer medicines.

Our composite model attempts to reconcile these studies. We assume that the first entrant retains an advantage over its "fair share," but the advantage decreases from +10 points to +4 points with additional competition. Beyond the first-to-market drug, our model splits the remaining share equally among the other competitors.

Compared with earlier models, our matrix of market share as a function of order of entry reflects slightly less dominance of early-to-market drugs over later agents. We think this is sensible for most modern biotech medicines, given the ever-increasing constraints on pharma sales and marketing activities (which, if unrestricted, would most likely favor the incumbents).

Drug-specific factors

Our matrix of market share assumes all other factors are equal, but of course they are not. Compared with incumbents in the market, new drugs may be objectively superior on efficacy, safety, or tolerability; clinically differentiated by dosing frequency; more competitively priced; or more aggressively marketed. Any of those factors could lead to more market share than in our model. Published analyses validate the general idea that best-in-class can sometimes surpass first-in-class. For example:

- Among calcium channel blockers and ACE inhibitors in four European countries, the positive effect of higher quality on peak sales was greater than the negative effect of order of entry.[90]
- In a study of 51 drugs across 13 classes, even third-to-market drugs were able to capture more than 50% of sales if they were superior to competitors. However, this best-in-class advantage decreased as the time lag behind the pioneer drug increased.[91]
- The econometric study of "me-too" drugs discussed above found that in the absence of clinical differentiation, speed to market and promotional spending were significant drivers of market share.[92]

For all that, it is hard to derive rules for how to adjust market share forecasts based on drug-specific factors. Occasionally, one can use data from comparators relevant to one's drug—for example, the launch of an oral or once-daily formulation within a class of existing competitors. In the absence of comparator data, we typically model the upside TAM scenario and the conservative share based on order of entry, as well as one or two intermediate scenarios selected to illustrate a range of hypothetical outcomes.

Adjusting inputs from primary market research

Even in early R&D, some biotech companies and project teams will conduct a small physician survey to determine the likely market share their drug might garner. Although a full discussion of market research methodology is beyond our scope, it is important to note that estimating market share from customers' stated preferences generally overestimates likely market uptake, because the survey data do not account for variability in the *intensity* of the intention to purchase (or in our case, prescribe).[93] In biopharma, it is not uncommon to adjust stated preference shares downward by 50% or more to incorporate them into forecasts and valuation models.[94,95]

6

LAUNCH CURVES

IN A TYPICAL BIOTECH FINANCIAL MODEL,** a drug's sales increase annually until they reach the peak defined by the addressable population and its market share, as discussed in previous chapters. Thus, to build the model, you need to define two factors: the expected lapse of time from launch to peak market penetration, and the shape of the uptake curve.

Despite the obvious importance of drug launch dynamics to both financial modelers and commercial teams, quantifying these factors remains challenging. Many existing analyses are outdated and use methods and data sets that make it hard to extrapolate the findings to the modern era. In addition, many biopharma investors and executives find it tantalizingly attractive to customize a launch curve based on the unique characteristics of a drug or market, rather than relying on a "typical" base-case launch curve.

Based on our independent research detailed below, experience, and analysis of prior work, we typically use a six-year curve as our base case for modeling the launches of early-stage drugs, with occasional customization based on drug- or market-specific factors. Below, we summarize data from us and others supporting this approach, and provide ranges for percentage of peak uptake by year to accommodate various scenarios.

Time to peak

The most widely cited launch curve assumptions come from an econometric model developed by Bauer and Fischer in 2000[96] and a related follow-up analysis.[97] They showed that "pioneer" drugs, or those first in a therapeutic area or class, have a slower uptake compared with "followers." In their analysis, pioneer medications took about eight years to reach their peak, compared with three or four years for followers.

However, these earlier analyses have three limitations for contemporary biotech financial models. First, the researchers studied drugs in just four classes of cardiovascular medicine—angiotensin converting enzyme (ACE) inhibitors, antiarrhythmics, beta-blockers, and calcium channel blockers. These are unlikely to reflect the broad spectrum of drugs today. Second, these analyses included both U.S. and ex-U.S. launches, without any correction for differences in market access or dynamics between countries. Third, the latest prescription data used in these analyses are from 1996, so the conclusions of the papers are at least two decades out of date.

More recently, we analyzed U.S. sales uptake curves of all prescription drugs approved by the FDA from 2000 to 2002, including data up to and including 2015.[98] Unlike the previous studies, we did not detect a statistically significant difference between "pioneers" and "followers." Instead, we observed that the median time to peak for the entire set of drugs was six years, roughly midway within the range defined by the earlier work. In addition, we found no significant difference between biologic and non-biologic drugs.

Shape of the uptake curve

The idea that innovations are adopted via an S-shaped curve—beginning with a slow phase of "early adopters," ramping up more quickly over time as adoption diffuses into the majority, and ending with a slow phase of adoption by "laggards"—was proposed more than 100 years ago. It has since been shown to be generally true across a wide range of industries.[99,100] Indeed, Bauer and Fischer's original launch-curve model for drugs[101] yielded complex equations to describe drug life cycles through launch, peak, and decay that appear to follow S-shaped curves, although there is insufficient information to allow one to extract the percentage of peak uptake by year for incorporation into financial projections.

In our analysis,[102] we also observed that drug launches follow a curve similar to an S shape. Rather than trying to define a mathematical equation to describe the shape of the median curve, we simply calculated the median uptake percentages by year, which can be integrated more seamlessly into a financial model:

FIGURE 6-1: Prototypical drug uptake curve.

% of peak

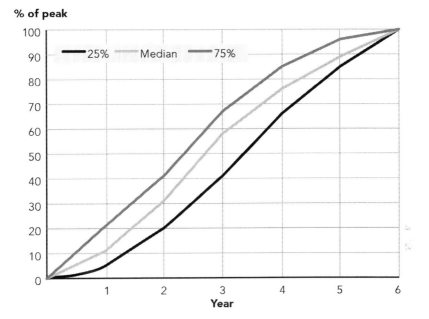

Year after launch	1	2	3	4	5	6
% of peak Median (IQR)	11 (5, 21)	31 (20, 41)	58 (41, 67)	76 (66, 85)	89 (85, 96)	100 (n/a)

Median and interquartile curves (top) and data (bottom) by year for drug launch with six-year time to peak. Adapted from Robey and David (2016); see text for details.

Of note, we found that the time to 50% of peak was just under half of the launch curve duration—in other words, the launch curve is slightly left-shifted.

Consolidated table of uptake by year

Because we did not observe a difference between "pioneers" and "followers," we tend to use the typical six-year ramp as the base case in financial models of both categories of drugs. However, there are situations in which one may want to forecast accelerated or delayed uptake based on the perceived level of demand for a novel therapy (in terms of the underlying unmet need, its points and degree of differentiation, and the projected market "pull"/receptiveness for the new agent).

There are other reasons why one might want to model ramps longer or shorter than the six-year base case. First, it is sometimes both attractive and practical to model the time to peak as mimicking that of an existing drug for which launch data are available. Second, it is sometimes appropriate to model future product line extensions or label expansions as a single "product family" with a longer time to peak, rather than attempting to forecast each launch individually. And finally, because valuation models are exquisitely sensitive to the "time value of money," it can be helpful in some analytic scenarios to understand how the net present value changes if one varies the ramp rate around a base case value.

Based on data from our work, we scaled the median and interquartile ranges for uptake by year across a broad range of ramp durations. The resulting sales ramp curves are summarized below:

FIGURE 6-2: Consolidated table of drug uptake by year.

		Year of ramp									
		1	2	3	4	5	6	7	8	9	10
Length of ramp (y)	3	31% 20–41%	76% 66–85%	100%							
	4	21% 14–30%	58% 41–67%	83% 78–91%	100%						
	5	15% 7–25%	42% 27–53%	68% 57–78%	86% 82–94%	100%					
	6	11% 5–21%	31% 20–41%	58% 41–67%	76% 66–85%	89% 85–96%	100%				
	7	9% 4–18%	25% 17–35%	46% 30–57%	66% 52–75%	80% 74–88%	90% 87–96%	100%			
	8	8% 3–15%	21% 14–30%	37% 24–48%	58% 41–67%	71% 60–81%	83% 78–91%	92% 88–96%	100%		
	9	7% 3–13%	18% 11–27%	31% 20–41%	49% 33–59%	64% 49–73%	76% 66–85%	85% 80–93%	93% 89–96%	100%	
	10	6% 2–11%	15% 7–25%	28% 18–37%	42% 27–53%	58% 41–67%	68% 57–78%	79% 72–87%	86% 82–94%	93% 90–97%	100%

Median and interquartile ranges of uptake by year for drug launches of various ramp lengths. Pharmagellan analysis based on data from Robey and David (2016).

X% = Median
Y–Z% = Interquartile range

7

LOSS OF EXCLUSIVITY

MANY BIOTECH FORECASTS cover a time range long enough to include the projected date of competition from generics or biosimilars. These sales are typically so far in the future that they will have a minimal effect on discounted cash flow valuations. Nonetheless, most end users of biotech models expect them to describe the timing and magnitude of decreased sales volume and price after loss of exclusivity.

In this chapter, we address three elements of modeling sales after generic entry:

1. Timing of competition
2. Sales after patent expiration
3. Price after patent expiration

Timing of competition

In the absence of specific information on a particular drug candidate's patent status, we typically estimate about 13 years from launch to competition from generics or biosimilars:

- Among 288 drugs that experienced generic competition from 1995 to 2014, the average duration of market exclusivity ranged from 12.2 to 13.7 years, with no obvious trend over time.[103]
- The median duration of market exclusivity for 175 products that first faced generic competition from 2000 to 2012 was 12.5 years, with an interquartile range of 8.5–14.8 years.[104]

One can attempt to estimate the year a drug will face competition based on the patent term and the effects of various legislative extensions, but this can be challenging without detailed input from the patent-holding company itself or experts in pharma intellectual property law. Key factors that are typically incorporated into exclusivity estimates include:[105,106]

Patent term: Drugs typically generate a family of patents covering composition of the drug, its formulation, method of use, and other factors. Patent information for R&D-stage drugs can sometimes be obtained from public databases such as the U.S. Patent and Trademark Office[107] or financial filings of publicly traded companies, but determining the key patent or patents that control the most likely period of market exclusivity typically requires expert input and is beyond our scope. Importantly, the statutory patent term in the United States is 20 years from the date of the application, not arrival on the market, so the time it takes to complete trials and obtain regulatory approvals often takes away several years of exclusivity.[108,109] Patent expiration dates for already-marketed drugs can be found in the FDA Orange Book.[110]

Hatch-Waxman extension: Since 1984, U.S. law has extended patent exclusivity for drugs to account for the long duration of clinical research and FDA approval.[111] In practice, newly launched drugs typically receive a minimum of five years of protection from generic competitors under Hatch-Waxman, regardless of the filing-based 20-year patent timetable.

Orphan drug exclusivity: Orphan drugs receive seven years of exclusivity after regulatory approval instead of the five typically afforded by the Hatch-Waxman law.

Pediatric extension: Sponsors can gain six months of additional market exclusivity when they perform certain pediatric studies.

Sales after patent expiration

Whenever it occurs, the end of patent protection means that sales volumes will decline. For small molecule drugs, we typically model a 90% loss of sales volume in the United States within a year after a drug faces generic competition, based on a recent study of agents that first had a generic competitor in 2013–2014.[112] This analysis showed an average reduction of 88% in unit sales 12 months after the first generic entrant, which was 93% for drugs with more than $250 million in sales the year before loss of exclusivity. The shapes of the curves suggested that the values at 12 months represent a plateau.

This average value masks a significant amount of variability, however. Retained unit sales can range from 0%–30% in the United States, influenced by the size of the market (and hence, the level of generic competition) and the degree of "brand loyalty" among physicians and patients.[113] And in Europe, retained sales by the originator brand may be as high as 62% up to 24 months after loss of exclusivity.[114]

Compared with small molecule generics, biosimilars have substantially less history in the market, so it's hard to define average curves for biologics after loss of exclusivity. We currently assume that biologic drugs will lose 20% of their market share by volume within one to five years of biosimilar entry, based on the following data:

- As of 2014, biosimilars captured an average share of 15%–21% for three biologics (erythropoietin, granulocyte-colony stimulating factor, and human growth hormone) in Europe since 2006, although there was substantial variation between countries.[115,116]
- Two biologics that serve as credible analogs for future U.S. market dynamics realized peak penetration of 17%–18%. Shire's VPRIV, competing with Genzyme's Cerezyme, reached this level almost immediately after launch. But Sandoz's Omnitrope, a rival to Pfizer's Genotropin, took five years to reach peak market share.[117]

Price after patent expiration

In the United States, we typically model a 25%–50% reduction in price after loss of exclusivity. For drugs that lost exclusivity from 2001 to 2007, oral agents' prices fell by an average of 25%–26%, and those of physician-administered products, by 38%–46%.[118] And for biologics, a healthcare investment bank estimated that the average agent will lose 60%–70% of U.S. market value in dollars within five years of biosimilar competition, and 50% of that will reflect price concessions.[119] In a study of 12 EU countries, however, prices of originator brands declined by only 0%–25%, even 24 months after generic entry.[120]

EXPENSES

8

COST OF GOODS SOLD

THE COST OF GOODS SOLD, or COGS, is a function of units, not dollar sales, but for early-stage pharma assets and companies, most people model it as a percentage of gross revenue. This approach is intuitively less logical because it makes COGS falsely dependent on price. And yet it's the accepted approach for these reasons:

- It's simple to explain to clients, internal stakeholders, potential investors, et cetera.
- There are citable references to support your COGS estimates.
- It doesn't require or assume any specific knowledge about the manufacturing nuances of a particular drug.

Based on published data and our own analyses, we typically estimate COGS as 10%–15% of revenues for high-priced agents (including most biologics), and up to 30% for lower-priced drugs (e.g., small molecules in primary care indications).

Individual drug benchmarks

To benchmark the COGS-to-revenue ratio for individual drugs, we analyzed financial reports of publicly traded biotechs with unpartnered assets. Many of the drugs in the analysis below are premium-priced, so we would expect the median values here to reflect the low end of the range in the industry. Notably, we do not see a significant difference between small molecules and biologics, suggesting that price, not molecule type, is a more significant driver of the COGS-to-revenue ratio.

TABLE 8-1: COGS-to-revenue ratios for single-product biotechs.

Company	Drug (launch year)	Drug type	Fiscal year	Revenues	COGS	COGS/revenues
Aegerion	Juxtapid (2013)	SM	2013	$48,546	$5,019	10%
Aegerion	Juxtapid (2013)	SM	2014	$158,373	$14,370	9%
Alexion	Soliris (2007)	B	2007	$66,381	$6,696	10%
Alexion	Soliris (2007)	B	2008	$259,004	$28,366	11%
Alexion	Soliris (2007)	B	2009	$386,800	$45,059	12%
Alexion	Soliris (2007)	B	2010	$540,957	$64,437	12%
Amarin	Vascepta (2013)	SM	2013	$26,351	$11,912	45%
Amarin	Vascepta (2013)	SM	2014	$54,202	$20,485	38%
Ariad	Iclusig (2013)	SM	2013	$45,238	$9,612	21%
Ariad	Iclusig (2013)	SM	2014	$55,720	$5,224	9%
Biomarin	Aldurazyme (2003)	B	2004	$18,641	$3,953	21%
Biomarin	Aldurazyme (2003)	B	2005	$13,039	$2,629	20%
Biomarin	Aldurazyme (2003)	B	2006	$49,606	$8,740	18%
Medicines Co.	Angiomax (2001)	SM	2001	$14,248	$2,110	15%
Medicines Co.	Angiomax (2001)	SM	2002	$38,301	$10,284	27%
Medicines Co.	Angiomax (2001)	SM	2003	$85,591	$22,749	27%
Medicines Co.	Angiomax (2001)	SM	2004	$144,251	$29,123	20%
Optimer	Dificid (2011)	SM	2011	$21,511	$1,526	7%
Optimer	Dificid (2011)	SM	2012	$62,417	$5,486	9%
Regeneron	Arcalyst (2008)	B	2008	$6,249	$923	15%
Regeneron	Arcalyst (2008)	B	2009	$18,364	$1,686	9%
Regeneron	Arcalyst (2008)	B	2010	$25,254	$2,093	8%
Regeneron	Arcalyst (2008)	B	2011	$44,686	$4,216	9%
Seattle Genetics	Adcetris (2011)	B	2011	$43,241	$3,115	7%
Seattle Genetics	Adcetris (2011)	B	2012	$138,200	$11,546	8%
Seattle Genetics	Adcetris (2011)	B	2013	$144,665	$13,759	10%
Seattle Genetics	Adcetris (2011)	B	2014	$178,198	$17,513	10%
Vertex	Incivek (2011)	SM	2011	$950,889	$63,625	7%
Vertex	Incivek (2011)	SM	2012	$1,333,458	$236,742	18%

Vertex	Incivek (2011)	SM	2013	$837,645	$88,979	11%
Vertex	Incivek (2011)	SM	2014	$487,821	$39,725	8%
Vivus	Qsymia (2012)	SM	2012	$2,012	$187	9%
Vivus	Qsymia (2012)	SM	2013	$23,718	$4,868	21%
Vivus	Qsymia (2012)	SM	2014	$45,277	$33,387	74%
				MEDIAN (all)		**11%**
				MEDIAN (biologics)		**10%**
				MEDIAN (sm. molecules)		**15%**

B: biologic. SM: small molecule. Seattle Genetics analysis excludes royalty revenue and costs. Source: Company 10-K filings.

Although the COGS-to-revenue ratio in many of the examples above fluctuates after launch, we generally find it is logical and accepted in forecasts of early-stage products to assume a constant value during the entire commercialization period. A higher ratio in the first year is typically due to anticipatory manufacturing to fill inventory and supply chains. However, some companies book this initial prelaunch manufacturing under R&D, not COGS, which artificially lowers their reported first-year COGS. Regardless, we find that this level of nuance is generally not expected to be incorporated into biotech forecasts of R&D-stage products.

Industry benchmarks

Published industry-wide analyses of the COGS-to-revenue ratio have focused on companies with broader product mixes that are likely to include lower-priced agents. Two relatively recent studies calculated the average COGS/revenue ratio at about 30% from a sample heavily weighted toward large companies with portfolios composed of small molecules.[121,122] A 2008 analysis by company type determined ratios of 26% for large pharma, 14% for large biotechs, and 52% for generics producers.[123]

9

SALES, GENERAL, AND ADMINISTRATIVE

SALES, GENERAL, AND ADMINISTRATIVE (SG&A) expenses are made up of "G&A"—the company's infrastructure and overhead—and "S"—the costs of commercialization, including sales and marketing. In a biotech forecast, it's possible to estimate sales and marketing expenses for an individual drug, but this is not feasible for G&A for two reasons:

1. G&A includes many disparate, ill-defined parts—so it is generally impractical to build it up from its components.
2. Almost all commercial-stage companies report a single value for SG&A—so it is impossible to obtain benchmarks for just the G&A component after launch.

In this chapter, we outline our hybrid approach to forecasting SG&A, which combines estimates of discrete sales and marketing costs with a more general view of the entire SG&A expense.

- In the R&D stage (when there are no sales or marketing expenses), we forecast G&A costs based on existing benchmarks from public biotechs.
- For commercial-stage companies above a certain size, we model the total SG&A cost as a percentage of revenues (based on industry benchmarks) and use that figure to derive G&A (less sales and marketing).
- In the immediate postlaunch period, we model sales and marketing costs directly and use these to estimate G&A expenses.

SG&A for commercial-stage biotechs

Although most publicly traded companies do not report G&A separately from sales and marketing expenses, we can use their SEC filings to give us a view of overall SG&A expenses. We analyzed the 35 small- and mid-cap drug companies in the NASDAQ Biotechnology Index and found that median SG&A costs were 34% of revenues in 2015 (interquartile range, 19%–55%).[i]

However, as one might expect, this ratio is highly variable when revenues are low and more tightly distributed when revenues reach a higher level. For large-cap pharma companies from 2012 to 2015, the median ratio of SG&A to revenue was 28%, with a narrow interquartile range of 27%–33%.[ii] For small- and mid-cap biotechs, the ratio appears to stabilize above $400 million in revenues, with a median of 34% and interquartile range of 26%–42%.

FIGURE 9-1: SG&A/revenue ratio as a function of revenue for public biotechs.

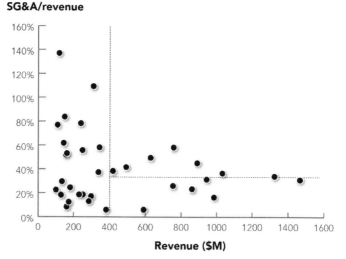

Pharmagellan analysis of financial metrics for 35 small- and mid-cap biotechs in NASDAQ Biotechnology Index. Data source: 2015 10-K filings.

---

[i] Pharmagellan analysis: For the 184 component companies in the NASDAQ Biotechnology Index as of September 14, 2016, we extracted 2015 reported revenue and SG&A data using Intrinio. We focused on companies with $100M to $2B in revenues, and eliminated those in the tools, diagnostics, or contract research sectors, leaving 35 companies in our analysis set.

[ii] Pharmagellan analysis of revenue and SG&A data from money.net from 2012 to 2015 for ABBV, AMGN, AZN, BMY, GSK, LLY, MRK, NVS, PFE, RHHBY, and SNY.

G&A for pre-commercial biotechs

It is impossible to model the G&A expenses of pre-commercial biotechs as a percentage of revenues, which are zero. So instead we rely on benchmark data from publicly traded biotechs that have not yet launched drugs. We found that the median G&A expense of 82 clinical-stage (pre-commercial) biotechs was $8.7 million (interquartile range, $6.3 million to $12.0 million), with much of the variability dependent on head count:[iii]

- Median G&A expense per employee was $225,000 (interquartile range, $168,000 to $398,000), and the median head count was 35 (interquartile range, 20 to 60).
- Companies with 20 or fewer employees had a median of $6.2 million of G&A expenses (N=26), whereas those with 70 or more employees had median G&A expenses of $14.0 million (N=18).
- G&A expenses appear to stay relatively constant across development phases with medians of $8.1 million for Phase 1, $9.2 million for Phase 2, and $8.7 million for Phase 3.

Modeling SG&A from prelaunch to maturity

We use the methods above to forecast SG&A in the prelaunch years and in years after revenues reach $400 million. To model SG&A in the intervening, immediate postlaunch period, we use the following approach:

- First, we model the projected revenues over time (see chapter 6) and identify the year in which they exceed roughly $400 million. From this point, we calculate total SG&A as a fixed percentage of revenues.
- Second, we forecast sales and marketing expenses individually (see chapters 10 and 11) in all years, as well as G&A in the prelaunch year as described above.
- Third, we derive G&A expenses in the "mature" years by simple subtraction.

[iii] Pharmagellan analysis: We collected G&A data for 82 clinical-stage (pre-commercial) biotech companies that had U.S. initial public offerings between January 2012 and December 2014 from 10-K filings and converted to constant (2015) dollars using inflation data from the U.S. Bureau of Labor Statistics. Companies with multiple assets were classified by the one in the most advanced phase.

- And finally, in the period from launch to the year in which revenues exceed $400 million, we linearly ramp G&A expenses.

To illustrate, consider a hypothetical one-asset biotech about to launch its first drug with the following inputs:

- Projected peak revenues of $1 billion in six years.
- Prelaunch G&A expense of $10 million.
- Sales expense of $50 million annually ($15 million in the prelaunch year), held constant for simplicity in this example.
- Annual marketing expense of 5% of projected peak revenues (i.e., $50 million), held constant for simplicity in this example.
- SG&A/revenues of 34% at "maturity" (>$400 million revenue).

First, we model the revenue ramp and calculate total SG&A as 34% of revenues in years with revenues of more than $400M:

TABLE 9-2: Modeling SG&A from prelaunch to maturity—step 1.

		L-1	L	L+1	L+2	L+3	L+4	L+5
Revenues		0	$106M	$315M	$580M	$762M	$884M	$1B
SG&A					$197M	$259M	$301M	$340M
	G&A							
	Sales							
	Marketing							

Next, we incorporate the inputs described above for sales, marketing, and prelaunch G&A expenses:

TABLE 9-3: Modeling SG&A from prelaunch to maturity—step 2.

		L-1	L	L+1	L+2	L+3	L+4	L+5
Revenues		0	$106M	$315M	$580M	$762M	$884M	$1B
SG&A					$197M	$259M	$301M	$340M
	G&A	$10M						
	Sales	$15M	$50M	$50M	$50M	$50M	$50M	$50M
	Marketing	0	$50M	$50M	$50M	$50M	$50M	$50M

Then, we input the missing G&A values in the years in which SG&A is being calculated as a percentage of revenues:

TABLE 9-4: Modeling SG&A from prelaunch to maturity—step 3.

		L-1	L	L+1	L+2	L+3	L+4	L+5
Revenues		0	$106M	$315M	$580M	$762M	$884M	$1B
SG&A					$197M	$259M	$301M	$340M
	G&A	$10M			$97M	$159M	$201M	$240M
	Sales	$15M	$50M	$50M	$50M	$50M	$50M	$50M
	Marketing	0	$50M	$50M	$50M	$50M	$50M	$50M

And finally, we linearly ramp G&A expenses in the early postlaunch years and add them to sales and marketing to calculate total SG&A in this period:

TABLE 9-5: Modeling SG&A from prelaunch to maturity—step 4.

		L-1	L	L+1	L+2	L+3	L+4	L+5
Revenues		0	$106M	$315M	$580M	$762M	$884M	$1B
SG&A		$25M	$139M	$168M	$197M	$259M	$301M	$340M
	G&A	$10M	$39M	$68M	$97M	$159M	$201M	$240M
	Sales	$15M	$50M	$50M	$50M	$50M	$50M	$50M
	Marketing	0	$50M	$50M	$50M	$50M	$50M	$50M

10

SALES FORCE

I **N MOST PUBLICLY TRADED COMPANIES'** financial statements, the sales expense is rolled into SG&A (sales, general, and administrative costs). When creating models for biotechs, however, it's common to create a separate line item for sales expenses. Doing so:

- Provides a level of transparency into commercial costs that most biotechs and early-stage investors like to see.
- Gives you the option of reducing the sales force cost to reflect partnerships or novel commercialization models, such as a low number of reps.
- Allows you to estimate potential synergies if a biotech is acquired and the larger partner puts the drug in the bag of existing reps.

In later stages of drug development, commercial teams typically model sales organizations as pyramids, perhaps including a VP, several regional managers, and a stable of field-based reps. They then calculate the size of the pyramid based on the number of physicians they're trying to reach and the geographic distribution, and also add a variable number of technically trained "medical science liaisons" to provide educational support to the sales reps.

But we find that this approach is overkill for early-stage biotechs. First, commercialization is very far in the future, so these sorts of sales force sizing models aren't appropriate for early-stage companies. And second, the typical users and consumers of financial models for early-stage biotechs aren't interested in this level of detail.

Instead, we typically advocate that you:

1. Estimate the size of the sales force for a particular product based on the drug's therapeutic area and call point.
2. Apply a standard "fully loaded" cost per rep.
3. Apply the sales expense over the commercialization period, including ramp-up in the prelaunch year.
4. Use the U.S. values to approximate ex-U.S. sales force sizes and costs as needed.

Sales force size

To estimate the size of the sales force to support a single product, we focus on the call point/specialty of the drug in question. For biotechs, these are most commonly the hospital, specialty physicians, or primary care physicians.

Hospital- and specialty-focused

We typically model a sales force of about 100 people to commercialize a hospital-based or specialty-focused product. This value is based on our analysis of product launches in which a sales force supported a single product. When possible, we customize it based on a specific, relevant comparator.

TABLE 10-1: Sales force sizes for single-product biotechs.

Drug (Company, launch year)	Indication (Target specialty)	Number of sales reps
Adcetris (Seattle Genetics, 2011)	Hodgkin's lymphoma; systemic anaplastic large cell lymphoma (Hematology/oncology)	60[124]
Ampyra (Acorda, 2010)	Multiple sclerosis (Neurology)	90[125]
Angiomax* (Medicines Co., 2001)	Anticoagulation during angioplasty (Interventional cardiology)	120[126]
Avenova (Novabay, 2014)	Dry eye; other ophtho disorders (Ophthalmology)	50[127]
Benlysta (Human Genome Sciences, 2011)	Lupus (Rheumatology)	150[128,129,^]
Cubicin* (Cubist, 2003)	Gram-positive organisms (Inpatient infectious disease)	180[130]

Jakafi (Incyte, 2011)	Myelofibrosis; polycythemia vera (Hematology/oncology)	60[131]
Juxtapid (Aegerion, 2013)	Familial hypercholesterolemia [Cardiology (lipidologists)]	25[132]
Northera (Chelsea Therapeutics, 2014)	Neurogenic orthostatic hypotension (Neurology)	85[133]
Ofev (Boehringer Ingelheim, 2014)	Idiopathic pulmonary fibrosis (Pulmonology)	200[134]
Omontys** (Affymax, 2012)	CKD-associated anemia (Nephrology/hemodialysis)	80[135]
Vibativ* (Theravance, 2009)	Bacterial pneumonia (HABP/VABP) (Inpatient infectious disease)	50[136]
Xtandi (Medivation/Astellas, 2012)	Prostate cancer (Urology)	180[137]
	MEDIAN	**85**
	AVERAGE	**102**

Hospital-focused. **Dialysis center-focused.
^ *Benlysta was supported by 75 reps from GSK and 75 from HGS; see references.*

Primary care–focused

The main challenge to estimating the size of a primary care sales force is that there are few single-product sales examples to serve as benchmarks. Most primary care–focused drug companies, which tend to be large or specialty pharma enterprises, have multiple products in the bag of sales reps. So it is hard to estimate per-drug sales support without additional data on the amount of effort reps are putting into each product. Of the biotechs that have launched their own single drugs, few have entered primary care. Many of those that have done so either partnered with bigger companies to leverage larger sales infrastructures or targeted a mix of primary care providers and specialists.

We typically assume that a biotech without partners will field around 500 reps to support a single primary care product. This assumption is roughly the median of several data points that illustrate a range of field force sizes:

- Large pharma companies—many of which are overweight in primary care indications—typically derive $1.5 million of revenue for each sales rep,[138] implying a field force of 667 reps for each $1 billion of revenue.

This may be an optimistic estimate for single-product biotechs in primary care, however, because large pharma companies gain synergies from selling multiple products.

- Pfizer reduced its U.S. sales force from 3,000 to 2,400 when Lipitor lost exclusivity, implying an effective primary care sales force of 600 reps for that single drug.[139]
- Astellas sold Myrbetriq for overactive bladder, together with another product, via a 700-rep force targeting primary care providers, ob-gyns, and urologists.[140]
- When AstraZeneca withdrew direct sales support from Nexium, it replaced 430 primary care sales reps with 300 call-center workers.[141]
- Somaxon launched its insomnia drug Silenor with support from 215–245 reps—including 105 from its partner P&G—targeting high-prescribing primary care and specialty physicians as well as pharmacies.[142,143]
- Ironwood deployed 160 reps (most likely targeting a mix of primary and specialty care) to sell its drug Linzess for constipation and irritable bowel syndrome, but this was supplemented with 1,300 Forest reps (who presumably also detailed other drugs).[144]
- Horizon supported its Duexis drug for RA/OA pain with 150 primary care reps plus "an undisclosed number" from Mallinckrodt.[145]

Additional illustrative data come from the highly competitive weight-loss class, where companies have deployed a broad range of sales forces targeting a mix of primary and specialty care:

- Takeda fielded 900 sales reps to support Orexigen's weight-loss medicine Contrave, of whom a subset also sold Takeda's other diabetes drugs.[146]
- Novo Nordisk said it would assign 500 U.S. reps to sell its weight-loss drug, Saxenda, to a mix of primary care physicians and endocrinologists, presumably together with drugs in its diabetes portfolio.[147]

- To support Arena's weight-loss drug, Belviq, the company's partner Eisai put in place a 230-person contract sales force (with one other product in the bag) plus a 90-rep specialty-focused force. But this total of 320 represented a dramatic reduction from the originally proposed 600-rep field force.[148]
- Vivus launched its weight-loss drug Qsymia with support from 150 primary care reps, and analysts expressed concern that this was not enough to optimize its commercial performance.[149]

A word about physician population sizes

It is tempting but ultimately unhelpful to think that the size of the sales force should be scaled to the number of target physicians. To illustrate, we've excerpted data from the AMA's annual report of U.S. physicians by specialty:[150]

TABLE 10-2: U.S. physicians by specialty.

U.S. physicians engaged in patient care (total, 2012)	643,507
Adult primary care	172,450
Family medicine	74,978
General practice	8,243
Internal medicine (general)	89,229
Cardiology	19,138
Dermatology	9,728
Endocrinology	5,428
Gastroenterology	11,265
Hematology (excluding heme-onc)	1,512
Infectious diseases	4,900
Nephrology	6,820
Neurology	10,321
Oncology (including heme-onc)	8,543
Ophthalmology	16,387
Pulmonology (including pulmonary critical care)	8,905
Rheumatology	3,924
Urology	9,093

Source: Physician Characteristics and Distribution in the U.S., 2012 edition, American Medical Association. Data reflect self-designated specialty and activity. Residents are excluded. Specialties listed are for adult care (not pediatric).

For specialty care, we have not discerned any obvious relationship between the maximum number of target physicians and the average effective sales force size. This is most likely because although the *total* number of physicians may differ greatly between two sub-specialties (e.g., 5,000 more neurologists than endocrinologists), the difference in the number of *high-priority target accounts* is typically much less. Top-priority targets would be heavy prescribers or influencers who allow sales rep access, and this group would probably be a small fraction of the total.

Ex-U.S. considerations

Outside the United States, there are scant data available for modeling the sales force in a similar way. Therefore, for models of early-stage biotech assets, we typically assume that the ratio of sales reps to addressable patients is constant across geographies.

Cost per sales rep

The per-rep cost for a biotech sales force includes three components:

1. Total compensation (base plus bonus)
2. Employment expenses (benefits, payroll taxes, etc.)
3. Other expenses (car, equipment, drug samples, etc.)

Based on several sources, we estimate that the 2015 per-rep cost for a biotech was $190,000 for primary care, $280,000 for specialty, and $300,000 for hospital-based:

TABLE 10-3: Estimated total cost per biopharma sales rep.

	Primary care	Specialty care	Hospital-based
Total compensation (incl. bonus)	$100,000	$170,000	$185,000
Employment expenses (30%)[151]	$30,000	$50,000	$55,000
Other expenses	$60,000	$60,000	$60,000
TOTAL	**$190,000**	**$280,000**	**$300,000**

Pharmagellan analysis.

These estimates are based on the following data points:

- A 2014 survey of 61 pharmaceutical companies found an average annual cost per rep (which appears to include total compensation and "other expenses" but not employment expenses) of $160,000 for primary care, $228,000 for specialty pharma, and $243,000 for hospital-based reps.[152]
- A 2015 survey of 3,500 medical sales professionals across all sectors reported average compensation (base plus bonus) of $158,000 in biotech, $134,000 in specialty pharma, and $116,000 in pharma.[153]
- Our analysis of self-reported data from 645 biopharma sales reps on Glassdoor reveals an average total compensation of $100,000 in a sample heavily weighted toward primary care–focused companies:[iv]

TABLE 10-4: Benchmark biopharma sales rep salaries.

Company	Avg. base salary	Avg. total comp	No. of respondents
Abbott*	$80,818	$109,141	31
Abbvie*	$75,185	$98,518	10
Actavis	$62,199	$157,748	13
Amgen	$103,022	$163,108	24
AstraZeneca*	$74,941	$102,160	28
AstraZeneca*	$68,586	$85,484	18
Boehringer Ingelheim	$67,427	$91,006	27
Daiichi Sankyo	$63,574	$85,073	48
Forest*	$66,214	$84,624	34
Forest*	$66,009	$91,973	25
Forest*	$55,742	$138,242	10
GlaxoSmithKline*	$73,207	$107,056	14

[iv] Pharmagellan analysis: We extracted average self-reported salary data manually from www.glassdoor.com (accessed December 31, 2015), based on a search for "pharmaceutical sales rep," "pharma sales rep," "biotechnology sales rep," and "biotech sales rep." "Total comp" includes base plus all reported bonus pay (corporate bonus, commission, stock, etc.). Analysis includes companies with at least 10 respondents and excludes contract sales organizations and advanced/supervisory positions. Note that Amgen, the only specialty-focused biotech included in this sample, reported a total compensation 60% higher than the average (which is weighted toward primary care companies).

GlaxoSmithKline*	$69,788	$92,237	12
Lilly*	$75,465	$93,762	69
Lilly*	$66,818	$87,105	38
Merck*	$74,855	$103,383	63
Merck*	$76,198	$98,776	18
Pfizer*	$82,458	$99,670	81
Pfizer*	$68,741	$103,563	15
Sanofi	$71,597	$91,569	18
Takeda*	$65,126	$105,725	27
Takeda*	$71,115	$93,888	12
Teva	$74,472	$99,718	10
WEIGHTED AVERAGE (n=645)	**$73,261**	**$100,407**	
RANGE	**~$56–$103K**	**~$85–$163K**	

*Pharmagellan analysis of data from Glassdoor. *Duplicate listings of companies correspond to redundancies within Glassdoor's database.*

Timing and growth of sales force expenses

We typically model roughly 30% of sales force staffing to start in the year before launch, to account for planning, training, and executive hiring, ramping to 100% in the launch year. Financial reports of biotechs that launched their own drugs typically reveal that SG&A expenses increase significantly in the prelaunch year, and some of these firms begin reporting "SG&A" (as opposed to just "G&A") at this time.

At loss of exclusivity, we typically model a complete elimination of sales force expenses. Although one could debate whether sales force support should be withdrawn earlier, in practice this event is so far in the future for R&D-stage biotechs that the decision has minimal impact on a valuation based on discounted cash flow.

To account for compensation growth before launch and subsequently, we typically apply the same compound annual growth rate of about 2% that we use for drug prices, consistent with several studies of recent compensation trends.[154,155]

11

MARKETING

PRODUCT-LEVEL DATA ON MARKETING COSTS are notoriously
difficult to obtain. As a surrogate, we leverage data for the pharma
industry as a whole and for individual companies.

Amount of marketing expenditure: We generally assume marketing expenses of at least 3% of projected peak revenues. We do not separate direct-to-consumer from direct-to-physician marketing activities. Instead, we assume that in most cases, the total spend will be largely independent of the precise split between the two.

Timing of marketing expenditure: We typically model marketing spending to start in the year of launch and last until the loss of market exclusivity. Although some commercial activities related to marketing occur before launch during Phase 3 and registration, there are only weak data to indicate how to quantify this in the context of a financial forecast.[156] So we generally assume that Phase 3 marketing expenses are accounted for in G&A and that marketing costs during registration are subsumed by the sales expense that we assign during this period. (See chapters 9 and 10 for more details.) After patent expiration, many large pharma companies continue to heavily promote branded "blockbuster" drugs,[157,v] but we do not believe such a strategy applies generally across drugs and drug classes.

Industry-level data on marketing spend

The best recent assessment of marketing spending across the pharma industry comes from a recent U.S. study that used data from QuintilesIMS and Kantar

---

[v] See Table 2 of cited reference; 10 of 25 top-selling drugs in 2014 were past patent expiry, but still associated with substantial marketing and sales expenditures.

Media to calculate various forms of direct-to-consumer (DTC) and direct-to-physician (DTP) spending.[158] Total marketing spend (excluding sales and samples) was 2.6%–3.1% of revenues from 2006 to 2010, with a slight downward trajectory:

TABLE 11-1: Marketing spend as a percentage of sales for the pharma industry.

	2006	2007	2008	2009	2010
Sales	$292B	$296B	$290B	$305B	$307B
Total DTC spend	$5.891B	$5.483B	$4.738B	$4.868B	$4.371B
Total DTP spend	$3.777B	$3.819B	$3.882B	$3.804B	$3.691B
Journal ads	*$570M*	*$494M*	*$392M*	*$320M*	*$326M*
E-promotion	*$356M*	*$415M*	*$497M*	*$532M*	*$525M*
Conferences/ meetings	*$2.851B*	*$2.910B*	*$2.993B*	*$2.952B*	*$2.840B*
Total DTC + DTP spend	$9.668B	$9.302B	$8.620B	$8.672B	$8.062B
DTC/sales	2.02%	1.85%	1.63%	1.60%	1.42%
DTP/sales	1.29%	1.29%	1.34%	1.25%	1.20%
(DTC + DTP) / sales	3.31%	3.14%	2.97%	2.84%	2.63%

Pharmagellan analysis of data from Kornfield et al. (2013). All values reported as constant 2010 dollars. Excludes detailing and sampling.

Pharma company benchmarks

A separate analysis of U.S. promotional (marketing) spend by individual pharma companies found that total costs were 3.2% of revenues.[159] These authors used QuintilesIMS data to analyze 2014 DTC and DTP outlays. In the table below, we supplement those data with 2014 U.S. revenues to calculate marketing as a percentage of sales.[vi]

[vi] Note that the data in the source cited above may underrepresent the total DTP spend of individual companies, particularly with regard to journal advertisements. The five top-spending brands on journal ads in 2014 each apparently spent more than $5 million—more than all but one of the total company-wide figures reported in the analysis cited above. Source: Top pharmaceuticals in 2014 by ad dollars spent. Kantar Media. February 23, 2015. http://www.kantarmedia.com/us/thinking-and-resources/blog/top-pharmaceuticals-in -2014-by-ad-dollars-spent. Accessed September 16, 2016.

TABLE 11-2: Marketing spend as a percentage of revenues for representative pharma companies.

Company	DTC ($M)	DTP ($M)*	DTC + DTP ($M)	Revenues ($M)	DTC/ revenues	DTP/ revenues	(DTC + DTP) / revenues
Abbvie	363.19	42.65	405.84	10845	3.35%	0.39%	3.74%
Allergan	247.82	32.44	280.26	4511	5.49%	0.72%	6.21%
Amgen	135.87	54.84	190.71	15396	0.88%	0.36%	1.24%
AZ	335.35	164.08	499.43	10120	3.31%	1.62%	4.94%
BI	124.10	72.57	196.67	6162	2.01%	1.18%	3.19%
BMS	224.40	68.53	292.93	7716	2.91%	0.89%	3.80%
Dainippon	191.70	40.10	231.80	1354	14.16%	2.96%	17.12%
GSK	112.55	88.32	200.87	8203	1.37%	1.08%	2.45%
J&J	257.51	153.02	410.53	17432	1.48%	0.88%	2.36%
Lilly	337.01	49.18	386.19	7860	4.29%	0.63%	4.91%
Merck	211.64	129.84	341.48	14214	1.49%	0.91%	2.40%
Novartis	12.95	132.49	145.44	12987	0.10%	1.02%	1.12%
Novo	60.95	69.79	130.74	7685	0.79%	0.91%	1.70%
Otsuka	108.14	59.02	167.16	3693	2.93%	1.60%	4.53%
Pfizer	1107.84	147.46	1255.30	17164	6.45%	0.86%	7.31%
Sanofi	20.54	62.34	82.88	12868	0.16%	0.48%	0.64%
Teva	7.56	54.64	62.20	10634	0.07%	0.51%	0.58%
MEDIAN					2.01%	0.89%	3.19%
(interquartile range)					(0.88%, 3.35%)	(0.63%, 1.08%)	(1.70%, 4.91%)

*Pharmagellan analysis of data from 2015 MM&M report and U.S. revenue data (2014) obtained from EvaluatePharma. Companies from MM&M report for which revenue data was unavailable were excluded from analysis. * Includes e-detailing, journal advertising, and meetings; excludes "traditional detailing," samples, clinical trials, and direct mail.*

Corroborating these data, a survey of 181 biopharma marketing professionals and executives found that the average total marketing budget in 2015 was $11.9 million[160]—or about 2.4% of sales, assuming average projected peak revenues of about $500 million.

Product-specific adjustments

Marketing spend depends on the nature of the drug as well as the strategic aspirations (and budget) of the company. With those factors in mind, we tend to adjust projected marketing spend upwards—to 5%–10% of projected peak revenues—in strategic scenarios that might be likely to need additional DTP and/or DTC marketing, such as the following:

- High competitive intensity
- Competition versus an entrenched legacy brand (especially if that brand is cheap or off-patent)
- Relatively low disease and/or drug category awareness
- Historically low-innovation clinical area
- Large, heterogeneous base of treating physicians (especially with primary care indications)

12

R&D

MOST BIOTECHS base their assumptions about the length of time required for research and development on comparisons with analogous projects and overall industry data. That's more efficient than trying to derive bottom-up estimates of development time and cost. And they use per-patient cost estimates to model expenses based on projected trial sizes instead of building budgeting templates from detailed clinical trial protocols.

In this chapter, we present the main data sources available to support model inputs for the duration and cost of nonclinical and clinical drug R&D.

Research duration and cost before Phase 1

In most biotech models, it is convenient to divide the research period before Phase 1 into two stages:[161]

- Discovery, encompassing screening, lead identification, and lead optimization.
- Preclinical, including toxicology studies and other activities needed to support an investigational new drug (IND) application for clinical trials.

In 2010, Paul et al.[162] analyzed internal pipeline data from 13 pharmaceutical companies to generate the most robust published report of the amounts of time and money required for these two stages. This table summarizes the findings:

TABLE 12-1: Duration of cost of research before Phase 1.

Phase		Median duration	Median cost (2008 dollars)
Discovery	Target to hit	1 year	$1M
	Hit to lead	1.5 years	$2.5M
	Lead optimization	2 years	$10M
Preclinical		1 year	$5M

Data from Paul et al. (2010).

Several other analyses corroborate these estimates, particularly with regard to durations:

- In 2012, researchers from the Tufts Center for the Study of Drug Development (CSDD) analyzed the time from "first synthesis" (which we interpret as the onset of lead optimization) to first clinical dose (or the end of preclinical) for 38 R&D programs. The data came from seven small and mid-sized pharma and biotech companies and covered projects for which the first toxicology study occurred after 2005. The researchers found a median time lapse of about 2.6 years with a mean of about 2.9 years.[163]
- A subsequent CSDD analysis of 106 pipeline agents from 10 pharmaceutical companies estimated the mean period from first synthesis to first clinical dose (as above) at 2.6 years.[164]
- A 2012 study of R&D projects at 16 global pharmaceutical companies found that the mean preclinical phase lasted 0.8 years and cost $6.5 million. The median expense was $5.0 million. The research also showed that the discovery phase before preclinical averaged 3.9 years.[165]

Clinical development duration

The time for a development phase consists of two components: the clinical trial itself, and nonclinical time, including protocol development, data analysis, internal decision making, and other activities. Our base estimates of duration by trial phase are:

Phase 1: 1.5 years
Phase 2: ~2.5 years

- 0.7 year nonclinical (constant across programs)
- ~1.8 years clinical (customized by program/therapeutic area)

Phase 3: ~2.5 years

- 0.8 year nonclinical (constant across programs)
- ~1.7 years clinical (customized by program/therapeutic area)

In the sections below, we outline the data supporting these assumptions and our approach to modeling clinical development time in different scenarios.

Base-case time estimates by phase

Our base-case estimates of 1.5 years for Phase 1, 2.5 years for Phase 2, and 2.5 years for Phase 3 reflect the results of several analyses performed over the past decade:

TABLE 12-2: Summary of published estimates of clinical development duration by phase.

Methodology (year of publication)	Phase 1	Phase 2	Phase 3
Analysis of 3,181 compounds in Pharmaprojects database (2006)[166,a]	~1.5 years (18 months)	~2.7 years (32 months)	~2.5 years (30 months)
Benchmarking data from 13 pharma firms (2010)[167]	1.5 years	2.5 years	2.5 years
Project-level data from 16 global pharmaceutical firms (2012)[168,b]	1.2 years	2.4 years	2.2 years
Proprietary EvaluatePharma data on 630 trials (2015)[169,c]	n.d.	n.d.	2.88 years
Benchmarking data from 10 pharma firms (2016)[170,d]	~1.7 years (19.8 months)	~2.5 years (30.3 months)	~2.6 years (30.7 months)

[a] Medians calculated from Exhibit 5 by Pharmagellan. [b] Time periods calculated by Pharmagellan from authors' reported data on durations from mid-phase to launch. [c] Median values. [d] DiMasi derives longer total phase times (with overlaps between phases); here we report the non-overlapping portion of each phase, for more accurate comparison with other data sources (which assume the phases progress in series, without overlaps). n.d., not determined.

Refined estimates of phase duration by therapeutic area (Phase 2 and Phase 3)

We generally find it unnecessary in biotech financial models to customize Phase 1 trial lengths based on the therapeutic area. A previous analysis found that in 8 of 11 therapeutic areas examined, Phase 1 duration was within three months of 1.5 years.[171] Not only is the distribution of Phase 1 durations relatively narrow, but such small differences are unlikely to have major effects on biotech valuations.

However, in Phases 2 and 3 we do customize estimates of the length of time based on therapeutic area because the distribution is broader and the absolute differences are larger and can lead to a greater impact on financial value. We do this in two steps:

- First, we determine the portion of total phase length that is due to nonclinical time, which we assume is constant across therapeutic areas.
- Then, we estimate the duration of the clinical portion based on industry benchmarks and/or specific comparators.

Nonclinical time estimates: We derived nonclinical time estimates of 0.7 year for Phase 2 and 0.8 year for Phase 3 by analyzing data from 9,125 industry-sponsored drug trials in clinicaltrials.gov.[vii] This study yielded median clinical durations of 1.8 years for Phase 2 and 1.7 years for Phase 3. We subtracted those values from the average total durations of 2.5 years per phase (see above) to obtain the nonclinical time portions. Notably, our data on clinical durations compare favorably with those from an earlier study of clinicaltrials.gov data (on 14,319 completed trials initiated from 2005 to 2009). That study found average clinical times from "initiation" to "completion" of 16 months (1.3 years) for Phase 2 and 17 months (1.4 years) for Phase 3.[172]

Clinical time estimates: We believe the most robust way of estimating the durations of Phase 2 and Phase 3 in biotech models is to extract the elapsed times of completed trials from clinicaltrials.gov that serve as appropriate comparators. Then we add the nonclinical time (0.7 and 0.8 year for Phase 2 and Phase 3, respectively) to calculate total phase durations.

In some cases, however, you may want to leverage or reference more general data on how clinical development duration varies by therapeutic area—but

---

[vii] Pharmagellan analysis: We collected data from clinicaltrials.gov for all Phase 2 and Phase 3 interventional, industry-sponsored drug trials that were registered from 2010 to 2015 and had reported results by the time of our analysis in early 2016. From these records, we extracted the dates of "study initiation" and "results reporting," and calculated the difference as the clinical time.

this should be done with caution. It's true that there are some areas of agreement across data sources related to clinical development time as a function of therapeutic area. For example, oncology and central nervous system (CNS) trials tend to be longer than average, and development of anti-infective agents is typically shorter. However, there are notable exceptions. For this reason, we tend to rely on comparator trials whenever possible to define trial durations in financial models, and only sparingly use more general assumptions by clinical indication.

Our own analysis of recently completed trials in clinicaltrials.gov shows a roughly threefold range of clinical durations from the slowest areas to the fastest:

TABLE 12-3: Duration of clinical portion of trials by therapeutic area and phase.

Therapeutic area*	Phase 2		Phase 3	
	No. of trials analyzed	Initiation to results (yrs.)	No. of trials analyzed	Initiation to results (yrs.)
Anti-infective	385	1.3	848	1.5
Cardiovascular	139	1.4	566	1.6
CNS	204	2.0	383	2.3
Dermatology	64	0.9	228	1.1
Endocrine	204	1.2	914	1.6
Gastrointestinal (GI)	84	1.8	244	2.1
Genitourinary (GU)	35	1.5	145	1.5
Hematology	286	2.4	267	2.5
Immunomodulation	108	1.3	409	1.8
Oncology	850	2.6	372	2.8
Ophthalmology	70	1.7	188	1.8
Other	251	1.3	427	1.5
Psychiatry	127	1.3	570	1.1
Renal	34	2.1	79	2.5
Respiratory	148	0.8	496	1.5
Weighted average		1.8		1.7

Pharmagellan analysis of data from clinicaltrials.gov. * Assigned by Pharmagellan based on keyword analysis.

An earlier study[173] examined total clinical development time (clinical plus nonclinical) across various therapeutic areas. For comparison with the data above, we also show the "clinical only" duration, subtracting our nonclinical estimate from the researchers' data:

TABLE 12-4: Duration of clinical development (clinical and nonclinical portions) by therapeutic area and phase.

Therapeutic area	Phase 2 (total) (yrs.)	Phase 2 (clinical only) (yrs.)	Phase 3 (total) (yrs.)	Phase 3 (clinical only) (yrs.)
Blood	2.7	2.0	2.8	2.0
Cardiovascular	2.9	2.2	2.5	1.7
Dermatological	2.4	1.7	2.0	1.2
Genitourinary	2.3	1.6	2.1	1.3
HIV/AIDS	1.9	1.2	1.6	0.8
Cancer	2.5	1.8	2.4	1.6
Musculoskeletal	3.3	2.7	2.5	1.7
Neurological	3.3	2.7	2.7	1.9
Antiparasitic	2.8	2.1	1.1	0.3
Respiratory	2.5	1.8	3.0	2.2
Sensory	3.7	3.0	2.5	1.7

Total durations from Adams et al. (2006); clinical durations calculated by Pharmagellan after subtracting nonclinical durations (see earlier table).

Two studies have looked at how the total length of clinical development including all three phases varies across clinical indications.[174,175] As discussed above, our benchmark for total clinical development time across all drugs and therapeutic areas is 6.5 years (1.5 + 2.5 + 2.5).

TABLE 12-5: Total clinical development duration by therapeutic area and phase from literature reports.

Therapeutic area	Total time Phase 1– Phase 3 (yrs.) Adams (2006)[a]	Total time Phase 1– Phase 3 (yrs.) Kaitin (2011)
AIDS/HIV	5.1	4.5
Anesthetic/Analgesic	n.d.	4.1
Anti-infectives	5.3[b]	5.3[c]
Blood/Hematology	6.9	n.d.
Cancer	6.7	6.6
Cardiovascular	6.6	4.5
CNS/Neuro/Sensory	7.6	7.0
Dermatology	5.5	n.d.
Endocrine	n.d.	4.9
GI	n.d.	5.7
GU	6.2	n.d.
Immunology	n.d.	6.3
Musculoskeletal	7.3	n.d.
Neuro	7.4[d]	7.0[e]
Respiratory	7.0	7.2

Times for Kaitin's data are medians; Adams's data (extracted from Exhibit 5) are presumed to be means. n.d., not determined. [a] Pharmagellan analysis of weighted averages of Adams's original data. [b] Antiparasitics only. [c] All anti-infectives except HIV/AIDS. [d] Neurology, musculoskeletal, and sensory. [e] Central nervous system only.

Finally, a complementary analysis examined total clinical development times across FDA reviewing divisions for 200 agents developed from 2004 to 2012:[176]

TABLE 12-6: Total duration of clinical development (all phases) by FDA reviewing division.

FDA reviewing division	Mean duration Phase 1–Phase 3 (yrs.)
Anesthesia, Analgesia & Addiction	5.3
Anti-infective	4.8
Antiviral	5.1
Cardiovascular and Renal	6.6
Gastroenterology	5.9
Hematology	6.2
Metabolism and Endocrinology	7.8
Neurology	9.6
Oncology	8.4
Psychiatry	6.6
Pulmonary, Allergy & Rheumatology	6.3
Reproductive and Urology	6.5

Data from DiMasi et al. (2014)

This review of data shows how we do not see enough agreement between various studies of clinical development time as a function of therapeutic area to justify using "general" assumptions. That is why we favor using data from completed comparator trials to estimate phase times whenever possible.

Influence of regulatory status

Based on available evidence, we do not generally adjust clinical phase durations depending on the nature of the regulatory pathway:

- A study of 630 agents that entered Phase 3 from 2000 to mid-2015 found no difference in the median length of Phase 3 between orphan and non-orphan drugs (2.89 years vs. 2.88 years).[177]
- A study of drugs approved from 2000 to 2009 found slightly shorter total clinical development times than cited above, but no significant difference between orphan and non-orphan drugs (5.2 years vs. 5.5 years).[178]
- A 2016 study of all 29 novel anticancer drugs approved in 2013–2014 found that the median time from IND filing (beginning of Phase 1) to submission of new drug application was 7.4 years for those that did

not receive breakthrough designation. The drugs that received break-through status (and were presumably permitted to forgo Phase 3 trials) had a median elapsed time of 5.2 years.[179]

Clinical development cost

The most common way to model trial costs in biotech forecasts is to apply a per-patient expense to the projected size of each study (defined from analogous studies and/or expert clinical input). We estimate per-patient costs at $114,000 for Phase 1, $181,000 for Phase 2, and $58,000 for Phase 3.[viii] In this section, we describe how we calculated those estimates and put them in context with other data.

Derivation of average per-patient costs: Many companies' internal costing models calculate per-patient, per-site, and per-trial costs. They do not account for other direct and indirect expenses, such as internal personnel and overhead, which must be accounted for in biotech financial models. The most complete published analysis of trial costs, including all of these relevant expenses, is a 2014 analysis by Medidata, a clinical trial analytics company:[180]

TABLE 12-7: Clinical trial cost by phase and therapeutic area.

Therapeutic area	Cost per trial ($M) in 2014 dollars		
	Phase 1	Phase 2	Phase 3
Anti-infective	4.2	14.2	22.8
Cardiovascular	2.2	7.0	25.2
CNS	3.9	13.9	19.2
Dermatology	1.8	8.9	11.5
Endocrine	1.4	12.1	17.0
GI	2.4	15.8	14.5
GU	3.1	14.6	17.5
Hematology	1.7	19.6	15.0
Immunomodulation	6.6	16.0	11.9
Oncology	4.5	11.2	22.1

[viii] Note that with the exception of oncology and some rare diseases, most indications will require two Phase 3 trials for approval.

Ophthalmology	5.3	13.8	30.7
Pain and anesthesiology	1.4	17.0	52.9
Respiratory	5.2	12.2	23.1
Weighted average	**4.0**	**13.0**	**20.0**

Data from Sertkaya et al. (2014).

To use these data to calculate per-patient costs, we obtained data on average clinical trial sizes by phase from clinicaltrials.gov. We extracted the sizes of more than 19,000 industry-sponsored Phase 1 through Phase 3 trials registered between 2010 and 2015 that had reported results at the time of analysis (early 2016):

TABLE 12-8: Clinical trial size by phase and therapeutic area.

Therapeutic area	Average number of patients per trial (no. of trials analyzed)		
	Phase 1	Phase 2	Phase 3
Anti-infective	40 (1,103)	126 (385)	404 (848)
Cardiovascular	35 (416)	68 (139)	410 (566)
CNS	30 (644)	60 (204)	295 (383)
Dermatology	30 (187)	83 (64)	355 (228)
Endocrine	42 (759)	102 (204)	368 (914)
GI	36 (361)	60 (84)	325 (244)
GU	39 (130)	100 (35)	388 (145)
Hematology	47 (916)	51 (286)	217 (267)
Immunomodulation	37 (228)	72 (108)	295 (409)
Oncology	27 (748)	46 (850)	383 (372)
Ophthalmology	37 (564)	100 (70)	345 (188)
Other	31 (3,319)	73 (251)	314 (427)
Pain and anesthesiology	32 (101)	100 (56)	256 (191)
Psychiatry	33 (211)	60 (127)	265 (570)
Renal	25 (120)	65 (34)	321 (79)
Respiratory	36 (217)	74 (148)	429 (496)
Weighted average	**35 (10,024)**	**72 (3,045)**	**347 (6,327)**

Pharmagellan analysis of data from clinicaltrials.gov.

The Phase 3 data are corroborated by a study of 257 new drugs approved by the FDA from 2003 to 2013. The study found that the average number of patients per Phase 3 trial over that period was 372. In the most recent five years of the analysis, the average was 464.[181]

Using the average trial costs and sizes by phase in these two tables, we calculate the average per-patient costs as $114,000 for Phase 1, $181,000 for Phase 2, and $58,000 for Phase 3. However, these average values mask a great deal of variability, particularly in Phase 1 and Phase 2—as can be seen if we use the data to calculate the per-patient cost for each therapeutic area:

TABLE 12-9: Derived per-patient clinical development cost by phase and therapeutic area.

Therapeutic area	Derived per-patient cost ($K)		
	Phase 1	Phase 2	Phase 3
Anti-infective	105.0	112.7	56.4
Cardiovascular	62.9	102.9	61.5
CNS	130.0	231.7	65.1
Dermatology	60.0	107.2	32.4
Endocrine	33.3	118.6	46.2
GI	66.7	263.3	44.6
GU	79.5	146.0	45.1
Hematology	36.2	384.3	69.1
Immunomodulation	178.4	222.2	40.3
Oncology	166.7	243.5	57.7
Ophthalmology	143.2	138.0	89.0
Pain and anesthesiology	43.8	170.0	206.6
Respiratory	144.4	164.9	53.8
Weighted average[a]	**114**	**181**	**58**

Pharmagellan analysis of trial cost and size data from earlier tables. [a] Result of dividing average cost per trial (across all therapeutic areas) by average number of patients per trial (across all therapeutic areas) from prior tables.

A striking feature of these data is that per-patient costs are highest in Phase 2 and lowest in Phase 3. We believe this makes sense if one considers some of the factors that contribute to per-patient trial expenses. For example:

- Earlier-phase trials tend to garner lower patient and physician interest than later-phase trials because of the perceived lower chances of personal benefit. Thus, recruitment can be more challenging and expensive.
- Earlier-phase trials tend to be more complex and expensive with regard to the number and frequency of visits, the use of ancillary tests, and the possible need for inpatient admission.
- Phase 2 trials in particular often include complex and expensive screening (molecular and/or imaging) to test various patient selection hypotheses.
- Phase 3 trials are generally optimized for high efficiency of site initiation and recruitment, which reduce per-patient trial costs.

Another notable feature of our findings is the broad distribution in per-patient costs by therapeutic area. This variability may reflect several other factors, for example:

- Low-prevalence patient population requiring additional screening effort and/or larger number of sites.
- Population with high clinical trial activity relative to the size of the patient population (leading to competition and decreased recruitment efficiency).
- Off-label agents (not covered by insurance) in control or experimental arms that must be purchased by the sponsor.
- Clinical area with low diagnosis rates, low patient interest in clinical trials, or other characteristics requiring more effort to enroll early-stage studies.

A specific illustration of the factors that contribute to higher trial costs comes from a 2015 analysis of Phase 3 expenditures that found a median per-patient cost of $54,000 for non-orphan diseases, compared with $157,000 for orphan indications.[182]

Contextualization with other per-patient cost data: Two previous studies report somewhat lower per-patient costs than those reported here, but we believe these differences can be explained by differences in methodology:

- A 2013 analysis by IMS Health using its GrantPlan benchmarking database reported per-patient trial costs (across all phases) ranging from \$6,159 (devices and diagnostics) to \$18,654 (oncology).[183] However, these data exclude institutional review board fees, comparator drug costs, and legal/importation fees. They also appear based on scant methodologic details to exclude company personnel and infrastructure/overhead expenses. In addition, these are worldwide estimates, and it is unclear how lower-cost venues were incorporated into the averages.

- A 2015 analysis by PhRMA and Battelle reported average per-patient trial costs of \$38,500 for Phase 1, \$40,000 for Phase 2, and \$42,000 for Phase 3, based on data derived from a market research survey conducted by a third party.[184] Although these data include some of the elements that are not present in the IMS Health study, they appear to exclude most human and infrastructure costs.

Contextualization with per-phase data: Applying the per-patient costs and trial sizes to each phase of development for a "typical" biotech asset yields estimates of \$4 million for Phase 1, \$13 million for Phase 2, and \$40 million for Phase 3. This assumes one trial each in Phase 1 and Phase 2, and two trials in Phase 3.

Notably, a recent analysis of clinical development expenses estimated much higher median per-phase costs of \$17.3 million for Phase 1, \$44.8 million for Phase 2, and \$200.0 million for Phase 3.[185] However, we believe these higher values (which are similar to those in two earlier analyses[186,187]) are not appropriate for incorporation into most biotech models:

- All three of these studies use aggregate per-phase data from large pharma companies but do not report the number of trials executed per phase, which is likely more than the minimum required for advancement and approval.

- The per-phase estimates in the most recent analysis were associated with extremely large standard deviations ($29.6 million, $50.8 million, and $153.3 million, respectively), suggesting a high level of heterogeneity that makes it difficult to know how to incorporate the median values into a biotech model.

- It is possible that these estimates reflect "fully loaded" pharma per-phase costs that are higher than those of third-party contract research organizations and small biotechs, which we believe are reflected in our analysis.

- Finally, a fourth cost estimate of Phase 3 trials only, which is also higher than expected, is apparently based on a proprietary algorithm incorporating per-patient per-year costs, but there is insufficient information provided to vet the underlying assumptions.[188]

Post-approval R&D duration and cost

After approval, many drugs incur R&D expenses for Phase 4 trials (often mandated by regulators), safety databases, and other uses. We typically use one of three approaches to incorporate this expense into biotech financial models:

1. For indications and scenarios in which we can identify a suitable comparator Phase 4 trial, we anchor our assumptions on its size and duration, and use Phase 3 per-patient trial costs to estimate the total expense.

2. If we believe Phase 4 studies will be required but cannot identify a suitable comparator, we either assume it will be similar to a Phase 3 trial or use benchmark data from the 2014 Medidata study cited above:[189]

TABLE 12-10: Average Phase 4 trial cost by therapeutic area.

Therapeutic area	Average Phase 4 cost per trial ($M)
Anti-infective	11.0
Cardiovascular	27.8
CNS	14.1
Dermatology	25.2
Endocrine	26.7
GI	21.8
GU	6.8
Hematology	27.0
Immunomodulation	19.8
Oncology	38.9
Ophthalmology	17.6
Pain and anesthesiology	32.1
Respiratory	72.9
Average	**26.3**

Data reported by Sertikaya et al. (2014).

3. Finally, if we do not believe a significant Phase 4 trial will be required, we typically model a low, constant R&D spend ($5 million to $10 million per year) for the remainder of the patent life, based on data from small commercial-stage companies with minimal pipeline activity:

   - Cadence spent $6.5 million on R&D in 2012, two years after approval of its sole product, Ofirmev, on a post-marketing pediatric study (initiated in the second half of the year) and activities to support additional regulatory submissions.[190]
   - Novabay, which launched Avenova in 2014, spent $6.0 million in 2015 to support postlaunch activities and minimal pipeline R&D.[191]
   - In 2015, Vivus spent $10.1 million on R&D, which included $3.3 million for a post-marketing study of Qsymia (launched in 2012) and $5.9 million for R&D overhead costs and share-based compensation.[192]

13

REGULATORY

IN CONTRAST to R&D time and cost, we find that in most cases it is overkill to customize regulatory phase inputs based on the features of a specific drug because the duration and expense are generally small. Thus, we typically incorporate "generic" assumptions into our models of early-stage assets as described below.

Regulatory duration

The most robust data on amount of time required for regulatory clearance calculate the period from submission to approval as about one year for non-priority review. We typically model total regulatory duration of 1–1.5 years, reserving shorter times for drugs likely to receive priority or "fast-track" status. Although some data suggest that some therapeutic areas (or FDA divisions) have shorter review times than others, these differences are small enough to be ignored in most biotech financial models. We based our estimate on several data sources:

- An analysis of 1,050 drugs with applications filed from 2006 to 2015, using data from BioMedTracker, found an overall time from filing to approval of 1.6 years, with a range across therapeutic areas of 1.1 to 2.0 years.[193]
- A study of all 188 novel therapeutics approved by the FDA from 2005 to 2012, categorized by the degree of innovation based on a previously published framework, found median regulatory times of 291 days for "first-in-class" products, 185 days for "advance-in-class" drugs, and 396 days for "addition-to-class" drugs.[194]

- A study of 257 new drugs approved by the FDA from 2003 to 2013 found that the average regulatory time from submission to approval was 0.99 years and that the length of time remained largely unchanged over the decade.[195]
- FDA researchers examined differences across divisions of the Center for Drug Evaluation and Research (CDER) in approval of drugs whose applications were received in fiscal years 2003 to 2012. They found that median review times ranged from 182 days (oncology, antiviral) to 427.5 days (dermatology and dental).[196] Those findings were in line with results from a previous analysis by the Manhattan Institute.[197] Much of the variation reflected differences in the proportion of priority or fast-track applications that each division received.
- A study by EvaluatePharma of 630 drugs that entered Phase 3 from 2000 to mid-2015 found median review times of 12.90 months for non-orphan agents and 10.09 months for orphan drugs.[198]
- The most recent data from the Tufts Center for the Study of Drug Development, based on 106 pipeline agents developed by 10 pharma companies, found that the average time from application to approval was 16 months (~1.3 years).[199]
- A 2010 model based on benchmarking data from 13 pharmaceutical companies, plus internal data from Eli Lilly, estimated the time from regulatory submission to approval at 1.5 years.[200]

Regulatory cost

Regulatory costs consist of two components: the filing fees required by national agencies and the expense for outside consultants or employees to prepare the application. In our experience, however, most biotech financial models incorporate just the filing fees and assume preparatory costs are included in G&A expenses.

In the United States, a complete new drug or biological license application filing currently costs $2.6 million, assuming one manufacturing site and one dosage form.[201] Fees in Europe[202] and Japan[203] are far lower (about $300,000 each). Although most regions require annual regulatory filing maintenance fees for new drugs, these small amounts (less than $1 million in aggregate) are typically ignored in forecasts of the on-market period.

VALUATION

14

R&D AND REGULATORY PROBABILITY OF SUCCESS

ALL BIOTECH VALUATION MODELS incorporate assumptions on the probability of success and failure at each stage of development and during regulatory approval. We base our modeling inputs on several recent analyses and summarize their methods and sample sets below to streamline the rest of our discussion:

DiMasi et al. (2010)[204] analyzed 1,738 new drugs that entered Phase 1 from 1993 to 2004, using data from the IMS R&D Focus database. Their analysis was restricted to drugs that were developed in whole or part by the 50 largest pharmaceutical companies by revenue in 2006, including agents that were in-licensed or out-licensed, and excluded diagnostics, vaccines, and "new formulations and indications for already-approved drugs."

Paul et al. (2010)[205] used benchmarking from 13 large pharmaceutical companies collected through December 2007 by the KMR Group, plus internal R&D pipeline data from Eli Lilly.

Hay et al. (2014)[206] gathered data from the BioMedTracker database on 5,820 phase transitions from 2003 to 2011, which comprised 4,451 drug candidates from 835 companies.

Smietana et al. (2015)[207] generated probability-of-success data from "lead indication phase transitions for all novel compounds (excluding reformulated products and biosimilars) recorded between 2007 and 2012 based on Informa Pharmaprojects data." The number of drugs analyzed was not reported.

DiMasi et al. (2016)[208] updated their 2010 analysis by studying 1,442 drugs from top-50 pharma companies that entered clinical testing from 1995 to 2007.

Smietana et al. (2016)[209] updated their 2015 analysis by extending the study period to cover phase transitions from 1996 to 2014. This study included more than 9,200 compounds.

Thomas et al. (2016)[210] used BioMedTracker data to study 9,985 industry-sponsored drug program phase transitions that occurred from 2006 to 2015. These involved 7,455 agents from 1,103 companies. This study's authors overlap substantially with those of Hay et al., and the methods of the two papers are similar.

Research before Phase 1

The main published data on success rates for preclinical research come from Paul et al. (2010). They estimate probabilities by stage[211] at 80% for target-to-hit, 75% for hit-to-lead, 85% for lead optimization, and 69% for preclinical development.

Clinical development

Industry-wide analyses

We typically assume base-case success probabilities of 60% for Phase 1, 36% for Phase 2, and 63% for Phase 3 trials. We based these assumptions on published analyses across a broad range of drugs and clinical areas:

TABLE 14-1: Summary of published analyses of probability of success by phase of clinical development.

Source	Phase 1	Phase 2	Phase 3
DiMasi (2010)[a]	65%	40%	64%
Paul (2010)	54%	34%	70%
Hay (2014)[b]	66.5%	39.5%	67.6%
Smietana (2015)	56%	30%	59%
DiMasi (2016)[a]	59.52%	35.52%	61.95%
Smietana (2016)[c]	55%	37%	63%
Thomas (2016)	63.2%	30.7%	58.1%
Median	**60%**	**36%**	**63%**

[a] Values are for "self-originated" molecules only (excluding in-licensed or out-licensed assets). [b] Values are for lead indications only. [c] Values extracted from figure in article by Pharmagellan, not explicitly reported by authors.

However, these percentages include failures both for scientific reasons and because of strategic decisions based on budget constraints or business direction. For biotech modeling, those probability calculations as a result may understate success rates, particularly in the context of licensing discussions. This concept is supported by an analysis of 812 oral drug candidates proposed for clinical development between 2000 and 2010 by four pharma companies (AstraZeneca, Eli Lilly, GlaxoSmithKline, and Pfizer). This study found that about a quarter of terminations in early R&D were for nonscientific reasons that, one could argue, are not always relevant to biotech valuations:[212]

TABLE 14-2: Reasons for project termination in Phase 1 and Phase 2.

Nonscientific reason for termination	Phase 1	Phase 2
"Portfolio rationalization"[a]	18%	21%
"Commercial reasons"[b]	7%	3%
Total percentage of terminations for nonscientific reasons	**25%**	**24%**

Data from Waring et al. (2015). [a] "No longer a fit with the company's vision, strategic focus, objectives, or business needs, excluding rationalization as a direct consequence of merger." [b] Including, but not limited to, "budget or resource constraints; merger-related divestments."

Based on these data, we sometimes use base-case success rates for Phase 1 of 70% and for Phase 2 of 52%, adjusting for the nonscientific failure rates. This may be particularly appropriate for biotech models developed for partnering purposes—under the assumption that an acquirer is unlikely to terminate an in-licensed program for nonscientific reasons. Indeed, DiMasi et al. (2010, above) found that the odds of success for in-licensed drugs in Phases 1 and 2 were each 16 to 17 percentage points higher than for self-originated products.

Success rates by therapeutic area

Depending on the strategic scenario, we sometimes adjust our modeling inputs based on the disease area—particularly for those in which several studies agree on the direction of change up or down compared with the base case.

We summarize below data from three investigations of success rates by therapeutic area. In each table, we list the reported probability of success for drugs in a particular therapeutic area, as well as the absolute difference between that value and the success rate across all drugs in all indications in that study's sample. We summarize Phase 1, Phase 2, and Phase 3 in separate tables:

TABLE 14-3: Phase 1 probability of success by therapeutic area reported in published analyses.

Disease area	DiMasi (2010)[a]	Hay (2014)[b]	Thomas (2016)
Allergy	n.d.	n.d.	67.6% (+4.4%)
Autoimmune	71.8% (+6.8%)[e]	67.7% (+1.2%)	65.7% (+2.5%)
Cardiovascular	62.9% (-2.1%)	62.7% (-3.8%)	58.9% (-4.3%)
Endocrine	n.d.	61.2% (-5.3%)	58.9% (-4.3%)
Gastrointestinal	67.5% (+2.5%)[c]	n.d.	75.6% (+12.4%)[d]
Hematology	n.d.	n.d.	73.3% (+10.1%)
Infectious disease	58.2% (-6.8%)	66.9% (+0.4%)	69.5% (+6.3%)
Metabolic	n.d.	n.d.	61.1% (-2.1%)
Musculoskeletal	72.4% (+7.4%)	n.d.	n.d.
Neurology	59.6% (-5.4%)	62.7% (-3.8%)	59.1% (-4.1%)
Psychiatry	n.d.	n.d.	53.3% (-9.3%)
Oncology	71.8% (+6.8%)[e]	68.9% (+2.4%)	62.8% (-0.4%)
Ophthalmology	n.d.	n.d.	84.8% (+21.6%)
Respiratory	72.5% (+7.5%)	69.4% (-2.9%)	65.3% (+2.1%)
Urology	n.d.	n.d.	57.1% (-6.1%)
ALL INDICATIONS (Phase 1)	**65%**	**66.5%**	**63.2%**

[a] "Self-originated" only. [b] "Lead indication" only. [c] Includes metabolic. [d] Excludes IBD. [e] Data reported as "antineoplastic/immunologic." n.d., not determined. Numbers in parentheses reflect difference from baseline (all-indications probability of success) reported by authors.

TABLE 14-4: Phase 2 probability of success by therapeutic area reported in published analyses.

Disease area	DiMasi (2010)[a]	Hay (2014)[b]	Thomas (2016)
Allergy	n.d.	n.d.	32.5% (+1.8%)
Autoimmune	49.0% (+9.0%)[e]	37.3% (-2.2%)	31.7% (+1.0%)
Cardiovascular	32.4% (-7.6%)	35.7% (-3.8%)	24.1% (-6.6%)
Endocrine	n.d.	27.4% (-12.1%)	40.3% (+9.4%)
Gastrointestinal	34.9% (-5.1%)[c]	n.d.	35.7% (+5.0%)[d]
Hematology	n.d.	n.d.	56.6% (+25.9%)
Infectious disease	52.2% (+12.2%)	45.9% (+6.4%)	42.7% (+12.0%)

Metabolic	n.d.	n.d.	45.2% (+14.5%)
Musculoskeletal	35.2% (-4.8%)	n.d.	n.d.
Neurology	33.0% (-7.0%)	34.4% (-5.1%)	29.7% (-1.0%)
Psychiatry	n.d.	n.d.	23.7% (-7.0%)
Oncology	49.0% (+9.0%)[e]	36.7% (+2.8%)	24.6% (-6.1%)
Ophthalmology	n.d.	n.d.	44.6% (+13.9%)
Respiratory	20.0% (-20.0%)	31.6% (-7.9%)	-32.3% (+1.6%)
Urology	n.d.	n.d.	32.7% (+2.0%)
ALL INDICATIONS (Phase 2)	**40%**	**39.5%**	**30.7%**

[a] "Self-originated" only. [b] "Lead indication" only. [c] Includes metabolic. [d] Excludes IBD. [e] Data reported as "antineoplastic/immunologic." n.d., not determined. Numbers in parentheses reflect difference from baseline (all-indications probability of success) reported by authors.

TABLE 14-5: Phase 3 probability of success by therapeutic area reported in published analyses.

Disease area	DiMasi (2010)[a]	Hay (2014)[b]	Thomas (2016)
Allergy	n.d.	n.d.	71.4% (+13.3%)
Autoimmune	55.3% (-8.7%)[e]	80.8% (+13.2%)	62.2% (+4.1%)
Cardiovascular	64.3% (+0.3%)	56.5% (-11.1%)	55.5% (-2.6%)
Endocrine	n.d.	79.2% (+1.6%)	65.0% (+6.9%)
Gastrointestinal	50.0% (-14.0%)[c]	n.d.	60.6% (+2.5%)[d]
Hematology	n.d.	n.d.	75.0% (+16.9%)
Infectious disease	78.6% (+14.6%)	69.7% (+2.1%)	72.7% (+14.6%)
Metabolic	n.d.	n.d.	71.4% (+13.3%)
Musculoskeletal	80.0% (+16.0%)	n.d.	n.d.
Neurology	46.4% (-17.6%)	66.9% (-0.7%)	57.3% (-0.8%)
Psychiatry	n.d.	n.d.	55.7% (-2.4%)
Oncology	55.3% (-8.7%)[e]	64.7% (-2.9%)	40.1% (-18.0%)
Ophthalmology	n.d.	n.d.	58.3% (+0.2%)
Respiratory	75.7% (+21.7%)	85.0% (+17.4%)	71.1% (+13.0%)
Urology	n.d.	n.d.	71.4% (+13.3%)
ALL INDICATIONS	**64%**	**67.6%**	**58.1%**

[a] "Self-originated" only. [b] "Lead indication" only. [c] Includes metabolic. [d] Excludes IBD. [e] Data reported as "antineoplastic/immunologic." n.d., not determined. Numbers in parentheses reflect difference from baseline (all-indications probability of success) reported by authors.

Within these broad categories, some specific diseases are widely regarded as having lower probabilities of progressing past Phase 3. For example:

- In cancer, Thomas (2016) found that an overall Phase 3 success rate of 40.1% masked a wide difference between drugs targeting solid tumors (34.2%) and those addressing hematologic malignancies (52.6%), with a range by cancer type from just over 10% (pancreatic cancer) to almost 70% (chronic lymphocytic leukemia).

- Phase 3 trials in Alzheimer's disease have a notoriously low historical success rate, with only one new agent approved from 2002 through 2012 of the 244 drug candidates that entered clinical trials.[213]

Success rates by molecule type

Several studies have found that biologics' clinical success rates are generally about 10 percentage points higher than those of new molecular entities (NMEs), across all phases:

TABLE 14-6: Clinical development probabilities of success by molecule type and phase reported in published analyses.

	Phase 1			Phase 2			Phase 3		
	All	NME	Biol	All	NME	Biol	All	NME	Biol
DiMasi (2010)[a]	65%	67%	84%	40%	38%	53%	64%	61%	74%
Hay (2014)[b]	66.5%	65.2%	75.1%	39.5%	36.4%	44.0%	67.6%	61.7%	71.7%
KMR (2015)[214]	n.d.	40%	53%	n.d.	24%	40%	n.d.	65%	79%
Smietana (2016)[c]	55%	49%	64%	37%	32%	43%	63%	62%	72%
Thomas (2016)	63.2%	61.3%	66.0%	30.7%	26.5%	34.4%	58.1%	48.7%[d]	57.2%[d]

All, overall probability of success. NME, new molecular entity (small molecule). Biol, biologic.
[a] "Self-originated" only. [b] "Lead indication" only. [c] Values extracted from figure in article by Pharmagellan; not explicitly reported by authors. [d] Both NME and biologic values less than total for all drugs because of contribution of non-NMEs and vaccines to total. n.d., not determined/reported.

Success rates by other factors

Finally, Thomas et al. (2016) found that drugs targeting rare indications tended to succeed more often than those for "chronic high-prevalence diseases," and that those incorporating biomarkers for patient selection fared better than those that did not:

TABLE 14-7: Other contributors to clinical development probability of success by phase.

	Phase 1	Phase 2	Phase 3
All drugs (baseline)	63.2%	30.7%	58.1%
Rare diseases	76.0% (+12.8%)	50.6% (+19.9%)	73.6% (+15.5%)
Chronic high-prevalence diseases	58.7% (-4.5%)	27.7% (-3.0%)	61.6% (+3.5%)
Selection biomarkers	76.7% (+13.5%)	46.7% (+16.0%)	76.5% (+18.4%)
No biomarkers	63.0% (-0.2%)	28.8% (-1.9%)	55.0% (-3.1%)

Data from Thomas et al. (2016). Only a subset of drugs in their analysis classified as either "rare" or "chronic high prevalence." Numbers in parentheses reflect difference from baseline.

Regulatory

Based on the median of several analyses, we typically model a base-case probability of success from the end of Phase 3 to launch of about 88%:

TABLE 14-8: Overall regulatory probabilities of success reported in the published literature.

Study	Regulatory probability of success
DiMasi (2010)[a]	93%
Paul (2010)	91%
Hay (2014)[b]	86.4%
Smietana (2015)[c]	81.5%
DiMasi (2016)	90.35%
Thomas (2016)	85.3%
MEDIAN	**88.4%**

[a] "Self-originated" only. [b] "Lead indication" only. [c] Product of 84% POS for filing to approval and 97% POS for approval to launch. Identical data reported in Smietana (2016).

Success rates by therapeutic area

We generally do not correct our approval rate assumptions based on the clinical area because of the lack of agreement among published analyses—and they disagree not just quantitatively but often directionally. For completeness, however, we report here the results of several studies of regulatory success rates across various therapeutic areas:

TABLE 14-9: Regulatory probabilities of success by therapeutic area reported in the published literature.

Disease area	DiMasi (2010)[a]	Hay (2014)[b]	Thomas (2016)
Allergy	n.d.	n.d.	93.8% (+8.5%)
Autoimmune	100% (+7.0%)[e]	75.7% (-10.7%)	86.0% (+0.7%)
Cardiovascular	65.7% (-27.3%)	89.6% (+3.2%)	84.2% (-1.1%)
Endocrine	n.d.	82.8% (-3.6%)	86.0% (+0.7%)
Gastrointestinal	80.0% (-13.0%)[c]	n.d.	92.3% (+7.0%)[d]
Hematology	n.d.	n.d.	84.0% (-1.3%)
Infectious disease	86.0% (+7.0%)	90.0% (+3.6%)	88.7% (+3.4%)
Metabolic	n.d.	n.d.	77.8% (-7.5%)
Musculoskeletal	100% (+7.0%)	n.d.	n.d.
Neurology	-3.0%	84.9% (-1.5%)	83.2% (-2.1%)
Psychiatry	n.d.	n.d.	87.9% (+2.6%)
Oncology	100% (+7.0%)[e]	83.5% (-2.9%)	82.4% (-2.9%)
Ophthalmology	n.d.	n.d.	77.5% (-7.8%)
Respiratory	80.0% (-13.0%)	95.2% (+8.8%)	94.6% (+9.3%)
Urology	n.d.	n.d.	85.7% (+0.4%)
ALL INDICATIONS	93%	86.4%	85.3%

[a] "Self-originated" only. [b] "Lead indication" only. [c] Includes metabolic. [d] Excludes IBD. [e] Data reported as "antineoplastic/immunologic." n.d., not determined. Numbers in parentheses reflect difference from baseline (all-indications probability of success) reported by that study's authors.

Success rates by molecule type

We also rarely adjust regulatory success rates between biologics and small molecules, because of a similar lack of alignment across published analyses:

TABLE 14-10: Regulatory probabilities of success by molecule type reported in the published literature.

Study	Regulatory All	Regulatory NME	Regulatory Biologic
DiMasi (2010)[a]	93%	91% (-2%)	96% (+3%)
Hay (2014)[b]	86.4%	81.6% (-4.8%)	88.0% (+1.6%)
KMR (2015)[215]	n.d.	90%	86%
Smietana (2016)	n.d.	94%	92%
Thomas (2016)	85.3%	78.0% (-7.3%)	88.4% (+3.1%)

NME, new molecular entity (small molecule). [a] "Self-originated" only. [b] "Lead indication" only. n.d., not determined/reported. Numbers in parentheses reflect difference from baseline reported by that study's authors, when available.

Success rates by other factors

Thomas et al. (2016) found that drugs with patient selection biomarkers had higher probabilities of regulatory success than those without (+9.2% vs. -1.4% compared with baseline), and slightly higher chances of approval for both "chronic high-prevalence diseases" and rare diseases versus the base case (+1.9% and +3.9%, respectively).

Hay et al. (2014) observed that although drugs granted special protocol assessments or orphan designation by the FDA generally have higher chances of clinical success across all stages of development, their regulatory success rates are similar to those of the overall cohort (-3.2% and -2.2% vs. baseline, respectively).

15

DISCOUNT RATE

IN THEORY, the discount rate in a financial model should be an objective measure of how much less dollars in the future are worth than dollars today. But in practice, the choice of a discount rate is more strategic than algorithmic and depends on the business context.

The two most common reasons to perform a valuation in biopharma are to help determine (1) whether to pursue an internal project or external acquisition, or (2) the perceived value of one's own project or company from the perspective of a potential acquirer. In both scenarios, the discount rate is more accurately referred to as the "hurdle rate"—that is, the minimum return on investment required by the current (or prospective) owner of the asset or company.[216]

So what is the "hurdle rate"? In theory, it should at least equal the weighted average cost of capital (WACC), which is the rate of return needed to repay equity investors and debt holders. The WACC of a publicly traded company can be calculated from its disclosed financials, and many biopharma analysts choose a discount rate in line with WACC values for comparably staged businesses. This typically yields values for early biotechs that are higher than those for mature pharma companies.

But for valuation models of early-stage biotech assets and companies, the WACC can actually overestimate the appropriate discount rate in some scenarios. That's because the required equity and debt returns that comprise a biotech's WACC are influenced by both its inherent financial riskiness (due to its size, financial structure, and other factors) and its odds of R&D success. But in biotech, we typically account for R&D risk separately by risk-adjusting the cash flows at various stages of development, so using a typical biotech WACC as the discount rate can lead to "double counting" the risk.[217,218]

In practice, we take several complementary approaches to defining the appropriate discount rate for a biopharma valuation model:

- In models we develop for large pharma companies to assess internal or external opportunities, we use a discount rate of around 10%, in line with both calculated WACC values and data on discount rates applied in this context in practice.

- In models of early biotech companies or assets developed to assess their value to a potential acquirer, we also use the large-pharma rate of around 10%, to reflect the likely value to the partner.

- When we help small biotechs assess the value of assets in their own hands, for either portfolio planning or external acquisitions, we use a slightly higher discount rate—typically 15%–20%, with higher values reserved for earlier-stage companies. We believe this range accounts for the higher cost of capital for these enterprises, but is still compatible with independently risk-adjusting the cash flows of the R&D programs. It is also in line with common practice in the biopharma industry.

Relevant benchmark data

Several published analyses, using complementary analytic approaches and data sets, consistently define a reasonable discount rate for a typical large pharma company as up to 10%, and for pre-commercial biotechs, up to 20%, depending on the stage of the portfolio. Except as noted, all of these analyses use WACC-based methods that incorporate R&D risk into the discount rate:

- A 2008 analysis of a set of discount rates for public drug companies (mostly from the companies' own financial reports) found a range of discount rates of 7%–28%. Companies with the highest level of commercial maturity generally clustered at the lower end of the range.[219]

- In the same publication as above, the authors calculated discount rates for a set of theoretical biotech companies with a range of four-asset portfolios, using a proprietary model, and derived a range from 12%

(one asset each in NDA, Phase 3, Phase 2, and Phase 1) to 19.5% (one asset in Phase 2, plus three preclinical assets).

- A 2012 analysis of 186 publicly traded biotech and pharma companies calculated the WACC as 8.7% for market-stage firms, 13.3%–13.6% for clinical-stage companies, and 17.7% for preclinical entities.[220]

There is also supporting evidence for this range of discount rates from analyses of real-world practice. In a 2011 survey of 242 biopharma finance professionals, respondents' ranges of risk-adjusted discount rates (i.e., excluding project- and company-specific R&D risk) were 12%–28% for "early-stage" biopharma companies, 10%–22% for "mid-stage," and 9%–20% for "late-stage." As expected, all of those were notably higher than the ranges provided for non-risk-adjusted discount rates.[221] A separate survey of 12 business development and finance professionals from large cap (>$10 billion) biopharma companies used a median discount rate of 10% for evaluating internal projects—and, in accordance with the approach we outlined above, confirmed that they used the same rate to model external transaction opportunities.[222]

Finally, in the context of biotech business development, it is worth noting that some pharma companies use the internal rate of return (IRR) of their current activities as the lower bound of the hurdle rate they would apply to potential acquisition candidates. A 2010 modeling exercise calculated the IRR of a theoretical small molecule drug as 7.5%, and that of a hypothetical biologic as 13%.[223] Subsequently, a 2015 analysis of data from 12 pharma companies found that the IRR for the group decreased from 10.1% (in 2010) to 4.2% (in 2015); individual companies' average IRR across a three-year period (2013 to 2015) ranged from -1.4% to 10.2%.[224]

ACKNOWLEDGMENTS

SEVERAL FRIENDS, colleagues, and experts provided input and advice on content and style at various stages of this project. Many thanks specifically to the following folks who expertly reviewed the near-final draft: Sarah Bobulsky, Bruce Booth, Mark Casey, Masha Chapman, Adam Feuerstein, Jim Geraghty, Michael Gilman, Craig Gordon, Scott Innis, Brad Loncar, Vincent Milano, Briggs Morrison, Alex Nicolau, Joshua Schimmer, and John Sullivan. Although we were unable to incorporate all of their excellent suggestions before the book went to press, their feedback has already formed the basis of our planning for the second edition. We're also particularly indebted to David Sable for generously writing such a thoughtful foreword, and to all of the past and current members of the Pharmagellan team for their encouragement and support.

Several people who were critical to getting this project over the finish line deserve special thanks. Our content editor, Bob Simison, generously lent his careful eye, well-tuned ear for language, and deep expertise in business journalism to this endeavor. Tracy Cutchlow calmly and expertly shepherded this project through its final production, and provided copious amounts of moral support throughout the process. Denise Clifton designed our beautiful cover and stylish interior pages. And Luke Timmerman provided critical advice when we embarked on this journey—and, most importantly, hid from us the truth of how hard it would actually be!

Finally, our deepest appreciation goes to Julie Lin for her unflagging encouragement, without which none of this would have been possible.

REFERENCES

[1] Box GEP. Robustness in the strategy of scientific model building. In: *Robustness in Statistics*. Cambridge, MA: Academic Press; 1979:201–236.

[2] Shaywitz D. McKinsey confirms pharma forecasts fragile; can industry learn to survive without them (forecasts, that is)? Forbes.com. October 6, 2013. http://www.forbes.com/sites/davidshaywitz/2013/10/06/mckinsey-confirms-pharma -forecasts-fragile-can-industry-learn-to-survive-without-them-forecasts-that-is/. Accessed September 29, 2016.

[3] Savage S. The flaw of averages. *Harvard Business Review.* November 2002. https://hbr.org/2002/11/the-flaw-of-averages. Accessed September 29, 2016.

[4] Holtzman S. On NPV, DCF and IRR(elevance)? Decibel Therapeutics. September 17, 2016. https://decibeltx.com/on-npv-dcf-and-irrelevance/. Accessed November 9, 2016.

[5] David F. In defense of pharma forecasting. Pharmagellan. October 9, 2013. http://www.pharmagellan.com/blog/in-defense-of-pharma-forecasting. Accessed September 29, 2016.

[6] Sahlman WA, Scherlis DR. A method for valuing high-risk, long-term investments (9-288-006). Harvard Business School. July 24, 2009. https://hbr.org/product/method-for-valuing-high-risk-long-term-investments -the-venture-capital-method/288006-PDF-ENG.

[7] Aswath Damodaran professional website. http://people.stern.nyu.edu/adamodar/. Accessed September 30, 2016.

8 Opler R, Garrett B, Langer J. Valuation analysis in pharmaceutical licensing and M&A transactions: A tutorial. Torreya Partners. January 2014. http://www.torreyapartners.com/news/publications.php. Accessed September 30, 2016.

9 Pullan L. Valuation of your early drug candidate. https://www.pullanconsulting.com/resources.html. Accessed September 30, 2016.

10 Bogdan B, Villiger R. *Valuation In Life Sciences: A Practical Guide,* 3rd ed. Heidelberg, Germany: Springer-Verlag; 2010.

11 Aulet, B. *Disciplined Entrepreneurship.* Hoboken, NJ: John Wiley & Sons; 2013.

12 Cook AG. *Forecasting for the Pharmaceutical Industry,* 2nd ed. Burlington, VT: Gower Publishing Co.; 2015.

13 Creating a patient-based forecast. Thomson Reuters. http://ip-science.thomsonreuters.com/m/pdfs/TPP-Forecast-cwp-en.pdf. Accessed September 30, 2016.

14 Cook AG. *Forecasting for the Pharmaceutical Industry,* 2nd ed. Burlington, VT: Gower Publishing Co.; 2015.

15 Creating a patient-based forecast. Thomson Reuters. http://ip-science.thomsonreuters.com/m/pdfs/TPP-Forecast-cwp-en.pdf. Accessed September 30, 2016.

16 Aulet, B. *Disciplined Entrepreneurship.* Hoboken, NJ: John Wiley & Sons; 2013.

17 Centers for Disease Control and Prevention. *Principles of Epidemiology in Public Health Practice, Third Edition: An Introduction to Applied Epidemiology and Biostatistics.* Chapter 3, section 2. http://www.cdc.gov/ophss/csels/dsepd/ss1978/lesson3/section2.html. Accessed October 19, 2016.

18 Reeves M. Course notes—Frequency and effect measures. EPI-546: Fundamentals of Epidemiology and Biostatistics, Michigan State University, College of Human Medicine. http://learn.chm.msu.edu/epi/content/epi_3.htm. Accessed October 19, 2016.

19 Haynes-Maslow L. Understanding the CDC's new report: What are diabetes incidence and prevalence? Union of Concerned Scientists. December 2, 2015. http://blog.ucsusa.org/lindsey-haynes-maslow/understanding-the-cdcs-new-report-what-are-diabetes-incidence-and-prevalence. Accessed October 19, 2016.

[20] Snyder EM, Olin J, David FS. Maximizing the value of diagnostics in Alzheimer's disease drug development. *Nat Rev Drug Disc.* 2012; 11: 183–184. PMID: 22378261.

[21] Fiore K, Fauber J, Wynn M. Drug firms helped create $3 billion overactive bladder market. *Milwaukee Journal Sentinel,* October 17, 2016. http://www.jsonline.com/story/news/investigations/2016/10/16/overactive-bladder -drug-companies-helped-create-3-billion-market/92030360/. Accessed October 19, 2016.

[22] Vaccarella S, et al. Worldwide thyroid-cancer epidemic? The increasing impact of overdiagnosis. *New England J Med.* 2016; 375: 614–617. PMID: 27532827.

[23] Osterberg L, Blaschke T. Adherence to medication. *New Engl J Med.* 2005; 353: 487–497. PMID: 16079372.

[24] Blaschke TF, et al. Adherence to medications: Insights arising from studies on the unreliable link between prescribed and actual drug dosing histories. *Ann Rev Pharmacol Toxicol.* 2012; 52: 275–301. PMID: 21942628.

[25] Shin J, et al. Primary nonadherence to medications in an integrated healthcare setting. *Am J Managed Care.* 2012; 18: 426–434. PMID: 22928758.

[26] Tamblyn R, et al. The incidence and determinants of primary nonadherence with prescribed medication in primary care: a cohort study. *Ann Int Med.* 2014; 160: 441–450. PMID: 24687067.

[27] Sikka R, Xia F, Aubert RE. Estimating medication persistency using administrative claims data. *Am J Managed Care.* 2005; 11: 449–457. PMID: 16044982.

[28] Blaschke TF, et al. Adherence to medications: Insights arising from studies on the unreliable link between prescribed and actual drug dosing histories. *Ann Rev Pharmacol Toxicol.* 2012; 52: 275–301. PMID: 21942628.

[29] iAdherence corporate website. www.iAdherence.org. Accessed September 30, 2016.

[30] Birt J, Johnston J, Nelson D. Exploration of claims-based utilization measures for detecting potential nonmedical use of prescription drugs. *J Manag Care Pharm.* 2014; 20: 639–646. PMID: 24856602.

[31] Dickson M, Plauschinat CA. Compliance with antihypertensive therapy in the elderly: A comparison of fixed-dose combination amlodipine/benazepril versus component-based free-combination therapy. *Am J Cardiovasc Drugs.* 2008; 8: 45–50. PMID: 18303937.

[32] Hungin APS, et al. Systematic review: Patterns of proton pump inhibitor use and adherence in gastroesophageal reflux disease. *Clin Gastroenterol Hepatol.* 2012; 10: 109–116. PMID: 21782770.

[33] Darkow T, et al. Treatment interruptions and non-adherence with imatinib and associated healthcare costs. *Pharmacoecon.* 2007; 25: 481–496. PMID: 17523753.

[34] Trivedi D, et al. Adherence and persistence among chronic myeloid leukemia patients during second-line tyrosine kinase inhibitor treatment. *J Manag Care Pharm.* 2014; 20: 1006–1015. PMID: 25278323.

[35] Agashivala N, et al. Compliance to fingolimod and other disease modifying treatments in multiple sclerosis patients, a retrospective cohort study. *BMC Neurology.* 2013; 13: 138. PMID: 24093542.

[36] Kozma C, et al. Medication possession ratio: implications of using fixed and variable observation periods in assessing adherence with disease-modifying drugs in patients with multiple sclerosis. *Patient Preference Adherence.* 2013; 7: 509–516. PMID: 23807840.

[37] Bae JP, et al. Adherence and dosing frequency of common medications for cardiovascular patients. *Am J Manag Care.* 2012; 18: 139–146. PMID: 22435907.

[38] Claxton AJ, Cramer J, Pierce C. A systematic review of the associations between dose regimens and medication compliance. *Clin Therap.* 2001; 23: 1296–1310. PMID: 11558866.

[39] Eisen SA, et al. The effect of prescribed daily dose frequency on patient medication compliance. *Arch Int Med.* 1990; 150: 1881–1884. PMID: 2102668.

[40] Iglay K, et al. Systematic literature review and meta-analysis of medication adherence with once-weekly versus once-daily therapy. *Clin Ther.* 2015; 37: 1813–1821. PMID: 26117406.

[41] Darkow T, et al. Treatment interruptions and non-adherence with imatinib and associated healthcare costs. *Pharmacoecon.* 2007; 25: 481–496. PMID: 17523753.

[42] Bangalore S, et al. Fixed-dose combinations improve medication compliance: a meta-analysis. *Am J Med.* 2007; 120: 713–719. PMID: 17679131.

[43] Rolnick SJ, et al. Patient characteristics associated with medication adherence. *Clin Med Res.* 2013; 11: 54–65. PMID: 23580788.

[44] Elkout H, et al. Adequate levels of adherence with controller medication is associated with increased use of rescue medication in asthmatic children. *PLoS ONE*. 2012; 7: e39130. PMID: 22761728.

[45] Andrews JS, et al. Real-world treatment patterns and opioid use in chronic low back pain patients initiating duloxetine versus standard of care. *J Pain Res*. 2013; 6: 825–835. PMID: 24379695.

[46] Peng X, et al. Utilization of duloxetine and celecoxib in osteoarthritis patients. *Curr Med Res Opinion*. 2013; 29: 1161–1169. PMID: 23777314.

[47] Cui Z, et al. Predictors of duloxetine adherence and persistence in patients with fibromyalgia. *J Pain Res*. 2012; 5: 193–201. PMID: 22792005.

[48] Zhao Y, et al. Comparison of medication adherence and healthcare costs between duloxetine and pregabalin initiators among patients with fibromyalgia. *Pain Practice*. 2010; 11: 204–216. PMID: 20807351.

[49] Zhao Y, Sun P, Watson P. Medication adherence and healthcare costs among patients with diabetic peripheral neuropathic pain initiating duloxetine versus pregabalin. *Curr Med Res Opinion*. 2011; 27: 785–792. PMID: 21303196.

[50] Birt J, Johnston J, Nelson D. Exploration of claims-based utilization measures for detecting potential nonmedical use of prescription drugs. *J Manag Care Pharm*. 2014; 20: 639–646. PMID: 24856602.

[51] Chen W, et al. Patterns of atypical antipsychotic therapy use in adults with bipolar I disorder in the USA. *Hum Psychopharmacol Clin Exp*. 2013; 28: 428–437. PMID: 23861367.

[52] Berger A, et al. Medication adherence and utilization in patients with schizophrenia or bipolar disorder receiving aripiprazole, quetiapine, or ziprasidone at hospital discharge: A retrospective cohort study. *BMC Psychiatry*. 2012; 12: 99. PMID: 22856540.

[53] Lage MJ, Hassan MK. The relationship between antipsychotic medication adherence and patient outcomes among individuals diagnosed with bipolar disorder: a retrospective study. *Ann Gen Psych*. 2009; 8: 7. PMID: 19226463.

[54] Hassan M, et al. Comparing adherence to and persistence with antipsychotic therapy among patients with bipolar disorder. *Ann Pharmacother*. 2007; 41: 1812–1818. PMID: 17925501.

[55] 2015 ASP Drug Pricing Files. Centers for Medicare & Medicaid Services. https://www.cms.gov/Medicare/Medicare-Fee-for-Service-Part-B-Drugs/McrPartBDrugAvgSalesPrice. Accessed November 3, 2015.

[56] Colorectal cancer: Dosing and usage. Genentech. http://www.avastin-hcp.com/indications/mcrc/dosing-usage#doses_and_duration. Accessed September 29, 2016.

[57] Walpole SC, et al. The weight of nations: an estimation of adult human biomass. *BMC Public Health.* 2012; 12: 439. PMID: 22709383.

[58] AMCP guide to pharmaceutical payment methods, 2013 update. Academy of Managed Care Pharmacy. http://www.amcp.org/pharmaceutical-payment-guide/. Accessed September 29, 2016.

[59] Medicaid drug price comparison: Average sales price to average wholesale price. Department of Health and Human Services, Office of Inspector General. June 2005. http://oig.hhs.gov/oei/reports/oei-03-05-00200.pdf. Accessed September 29, 2016.

[60] Medicaid drug price comparison: Average sales price to average wholesale price. Department of Health and Human Services, Office of Inspector General. June 2005. http://oig.hhs.gov/oei/reports/oei-03-05-00200.pdf. Accessed September 29, 2016.

[61] Curtiss FR, Lettrich P, Fairman KA. What is the price benchmark to replace average wholesale price (AWP)? *J Managed Care Pharm.* 2010; 16: 492–501. PMID: 20726678.

[62] Fein, AJ. Transparency is here! CMS exposes pharmacy prescription profit margins. October 9, 2012. http://www.drugchannels.net/2012/10/transparency-is-here-cms-exposes.html. Accessed November 3, 2015.

[63] 340B Drug Pricing Program. U.S. Health Resources and Services Administration. http://www.hrsa.gov/opa. Accessed November 21, 2016.

[64] Medicare Part B Drug Average Sales Price. Centers for Medicare & Medicaid Services. https://www.cms.gov/Medicare/Medicare-Fee-for-Service-Part-B-Drugs/McrPartBDrugAvgSalesPrice. Accessed September 29, 2016.

[65] Pharmacy pricing: National average drug acquisition cost. Medicaid.gov. http://www.medicaid.gov/Medicaid-CHIP-Program-Information/By-Topics/Benefits/Prescription-Drugs/Pharmacy-Pricing.html. Accessed September 29, 2016.

[66] Bruen B, Young K. Paying for prescribed drugs in Medicaid: Current policy and upcoming changes. Kaiser Family Foundation. 2014. http://kff.org/report-section/paying-for-prescribed-drugs-in-medicaid-current-policy-and-upcoming-changes-comparing-pricing-under-different-measures-8593/. Accessed September 29, 2016.

[67] Medi-Span Price Rx. Wolters Kluwer. http://www.wolterskluwercdi.com/price-rx/. Accessed September 29, 2016.

[68] Red Book. Truven Health Analytics. http://micromedex.com/products/product-suites/clinical-knowledge/redbook. Accessed September 29, 2016.

[69] Survey of retail prices. Medicaid.gov. http://www.medicaid.gov/medicaid-chip-program-information/by-topics/benefits/prescription-drugs/survey-of-retail-prices.html. Accessed September 29, 2016.

[70] Aitken M. Medicines use and spending in the U.S.: A review of 2015 and outlook to 2020. IMS Institute for Healthcare Informatics. April 2016. http://www.imshealth.com/en/thought-leadership/ims-institute/reports/medicines-use-and-spending-in-the-us-a-review-of-2015-and-outlook-to-2020. Accessed October 14, 2016.

[71] Mehrotra R, et al. Global biotechnology—An outlook for 2015. Credit Suisse Equity Research. December 11, 2014. https://doc.research-and-analytics.csfb.com/docView?language=ENG&format=PDF&source_id=csplusresearchcp&document_id=1041851381&serialid=gyOw5w61cb3eYmsHs5Zz4aqQdVC2T4Hlcl06jpEZcg0%3D. Accessed October 24, 2016.

[72] Schondelmeyer SW, Purvis L. Trends in retail prices of brand name prescription drugs widely used by older Americans, 2006 to 2013. AARP Public Policy Institute. February 2016. http://www.aarp.org/health/drugs-supplements/info-08-2010/rx_price_watch.html. Accessed September 29, 2016.

[73] Canipe C, Walker J. How drug company revenue is driven by price increases. *Wall Street Journal*. October 5, 2015. http://graphics.wsj.com/price-hike-2015/. Accessed September 29, 2016.

[74] Developments in the prescription drug market: Oversight. Hearing of the Full House Committee on Oversight and Government Reform. U.S. House of Representatives. February 4, 2016. https://oversight.house.gov/hearing/developments-in-the-prescription-drug-market-oversight/. Accessed September 29, 2016.

[75] Ruggeri K, Nolte E. Pharmaceutical pricing: The use of external reference pricing. RAND Corporation. 2013. http://www.rand.org/pubs/research_reports/RR240.html. Accessed November 7, 2016.

[76] Bell GK, Rankin P, Wilsdon T. Global pricing strategies for pharmaceutical product launches. Charles River Associates. 2003. http://www.crai.com/publication/global-pricing-strategies-pharmaceutical-product-launches. Accessed November 7, 2016.

[77] O'Neill P, et al. International comparisons of medicines prices: 2011 indices. Office of Health Economics. October 2012. https://www.ohe.org/publications/international-comparisons-medicines-prices-2011-indices. Accessed September 29, 2016.

[78] Japan Sales, Volume, Pricing 2015. EvaluatePharma. March 2015. http://www.evaluategroup.com/public/Reports/EvaluatePharma-Japan-Sales-Volume-Pricing-2015.aspx. Accessed September 29, 2016.

[79] Pharmaceutical pricing policies in a global market. Organisation for Economic Co-operation and Development. 2008. http://www.oecd.org/els/pharmaceutical-pricing-policies-in-a-global-market.htm. Accessed September 29, 2016.

[80] National prices sources. Health Action International. http://www.haiweb.org/medicineprices/national-medicine-prices-sources.php. Accessed September 29, 2016.

[81] ZenRx corporate website. www.zenrx.org. Accessed September 29, 2016.

[82] Van Dongen S. Websites reporting medicine prices: a comparative analysis. Utrecht/WHO Collaborating Centre for Pharmaceutical Policy and Regulation. 2010. http://www.pharmaceuticalpolicy.nl/result/websites-reporting-medicine-prices-a-comparative-analysis/. Accessed September 29, 2016.

[83] The pharmaceutical price regulation scheme 2014. U.K. Department of Health and Association of the British Pharmaceutical Industry. https://www.gov.uk/government/publications/pharmaceutical-price-regulation-scheme-2014. Accessed September 29, 2016.

[84] Thomas A. Germany mulls limiting prices drug firms can charge to health system. *Wall Street Journal*. April 22, 2016. http://www.wsj.com/articles/germany-mulls-limiting-prices-drug-firms-can-charge-to-health-system-1461307437. Accessed September 29, 2016.

[85] Japan Sales, Volume, Pricing 2015. EvaluatePharma. March 2015. http://www.evaluategroup.com/public/Reports/EvaluatePharma-Japan-Sales -Volume-Pricing-2015.aspx. Accessed September 29, 2016.

[86] Kalyanaram G, Robinson WT, Urban GL. Order of market entry: Established empirical generalizations, emerging empirical generalizations, and future research. *Marketing Sci.* 1995; 14: G212–G221. DOI: 10.1287/mksc.14.3.G212.

[87] Cha M, Yu F. Pharma's first-to-market advantage. McKinsey & Company. 2014. http://www.mckinsey.com/industries/pharmaceuticals-and-medical-products/ our-insights/pharmas-first-to-market-advantage. Accessed September 30, 2016.

[88] Regnier SA, Ridley DB. Forecasting market share in the US pharmaceutical market. *Nat Rev Drug Disc.* 2015; 14: 594–595. PMID: 26272192.

[89] About HAS. Haute Autorité de Santé. http://www.has-sante.fr/portail/ jcms/r_1455134/en/about-has. Accessed August 30, 2016.

[90] Fischer M, Leeflang PSH, Verhoef PC. Drivers of peak sales for pharmaceutical brands. *Quant Mark Econ.* 2010; 8: 429–460. DOI: 10.1007/s11129-010-9089-5.

[91] Schulze U, Ringel M. What matters most in commercial success: first-in-class or best-in-class? *Nat Rev Drug Disc.* 2013; 12: 419–420. PMID: 23722339.

[92] Regnier SA, Ridley DB. Forecasting market share in the US pharmaceutical market. *Nat Rev Drug Disc.* 2015; 14: 594–595. PMID: 26272192.

[93] Jamieson LF, Bass FM. Adjusting stated intention measures to predict trial purchase of new products: a comparison of models and methods. *J Marketing Res.* 1989; 26: 336–345. DOI: 10.2307/3172905. Accessed November 9, 2016.

[94] Johnson T. Forecasting in practice: the art and science of adjusting preference share. Kantar Health. September 2011. www.kantarhealth.com/docs/white-papers/kantar_ health_white_paper_forecasting-11. Accessed November 9, 2016.

[95] Morneau K. Market research meets market reality: a dynamic approach to discounting physician preference share. Ipsos Healthcare. 2011. http://www.ipsos-na.com/knowledge-ideas/marketing/points-of-view/?q=market -research-meets-market-reality. Accessed November 9, 2016.

[96] Bauer HH, Fischer M. Product life cycle patterns for pharmaceuticals and their impact on R&D profitability of late mover products. *Int Business Rev.* 2000; 9(6): 703–725. DOI: 10.1016/S0969-5931(00)00028-7.

[97] Fischer M, Leeflang PSH, Verhoef PC. Drivers of peak sales for pharmaceutical brands. *Quant Mark Econ.* 2010; 8: 429–460. DOI: 10.1007/s11129-010-9089-5.

[98] Robey S, David FS. Drug launch curves in the modern era. *Nat Rev Drug Disc.* In press. 2016.

[99] Rogers, E. M. *Diffusion of Innovations.* Third Edition. New York: The Free Press; 1983.

[100] Kinnunen J. Gabriel Tarde as a Founding Father of Innovation Diffusion Research. *Acta Sociologica.* 1996; 39(4): 431–442. DOI: 10.1177/000169939603900404.

[101] Bauer HH, Fischer M. Product life cycle patterns for pharmaceuticals and their impact on R&D profitability of late mover products. *Int Business Rev.* 2000; 9(6): 703–725. DOI: 10.1016/S0969-5931(00)00028-7.

[102] Robey S, David FS. Drug launch curves in the modern era. *Nat Rev Drug Disc.* In press. 2016.

[103] Grabowski H, et al. Updated trends in US brand-name and generic drug competition. *J Med Econ.* 2016; 19(9): 836–44. PMID: 27064194.

[104] Wang B, Liu J, Kesselheim AS. Variations in time of market exclusivity among top-selling prescription drugs in the United States. *JAMA Int Med.* 2015; 175(4): 635–637. PMID: 25664700.

[105] FDA/CDER SBIA Chronicles: Patents and exclusivity. May 19, 2015. http://www.fda.gov/downloads/Drugs/DevelopmentApprovalProcess/SmallBusinessAssistance/UCM447307.pdf. Accessed August 19, 2016.

[106] Frequently asked questions on patents and exclusivity. U.S. Food and Drug Administration. http://www.fda.gov/Drugs/DevelopmentApprovalProcess/ucm079031.htm. Accessed August 20, 2016.

[107] U.S. Patent and Trademark Office website. http://patft.uspto.gov/. Accessed August 20, 2016.

[108] 2701—Patent term. U.S. Patent and Trademark Office. https://www.uspto.gov/web/offices/pac/mpep/s2701.html. Accessed August 20, 2016.

[109] Calculating U.S. expiry dates. GenericsWeb. www.genericsweb.com/Calculating_US_expiry_dates.pdf. Accessed August 20, 2016.

[110] Orange Book: Approved drug products with therapeutic equivalence evaluations. U.S. Food and Drug Administration. http://www.accessdata.fda.gov/scripts/cder/ob/default.cfm. Accessed August 19, 2016.

[111] Kesselheim AS, Darrow JJ. Hatch-Waxman turns 30: Do we need a re-designed approach for the modern era? *Yale Journal of Health Policy, Law, and Ethics.* 2015; 15(2): Article 2. http://digitalcommons.law.yale.edu/yjhple/vol15/iss2/2. Accessed August 19, 2016.

[112] Grabowski H, Long G, Mortimer R, Boyo A. Updated trends in US brand-name and generic drug competition. *J Med Econ.* 2016; 19(9): 836–44. PMID: 27064194.

[113] Matthews A, David D, Aroy J. Ahead of the curve: managing product lifecycle. *Pharmaceutical Executive.* June 2011. http://www.pharmexec.com/managing-product-lifecycle. Accessed November 8, 2016.

[114] Kanavos P. Measuring performance in off-patent drug markets: a methodological framework and empirical evidence from twelve EU Member States. *Health Policy.* 2014; 118: 229–241. PMID: 252014533.

[115] The impact of biosimilar competition. IMS Health. November 2015. http://ec.europa.eu/DocsRoom/documents/14547/attachments/1/translations/en/renditions/native. Accessed August 22, 2016.

[116] Grabowski H, Guha R, Salgado M. Biosimilar competition: Lessons from Europe. *Nat Rev Drug Disc.* 2014; 13: 99–100. PMID: 24445562.

[117] Kulich J, Jin E. How biosimilars track a unique sales path: Three case studies to help anticipate biosimilar sales entry in your market. ZS Associates. 2014. http://www.zsassociates.com/publications/whitepapers/how-biosimilars-track-a-unique-sales-path-case-studies-to-anticipate-biosimilar-entry-in-your-market.aspx. Accessed August 22, 2016.

[118] Conti RM, Berndt ER. Specialty drug prices and utilization after loss of U.S. patent exclusivity, 2001–2007. National Bureau of Economic Research, Working Paper 20016. 2014. http://www.nber.org/papers/w20016. Accessed August 22, 2016.

[119] Citi GPS: Global Perspectives and Solutions. Disruptive innovations III—Ten more things to stop and think about. Citigroup. July 2015. https://www.citivelocity.com/citigps/ReportSeries.action?recordId=40. Accessed August 22, 2016.

[120] Kanavos P. Measuring performance in off-patent drug markets: a methodological framework and empirical evidence from twelve EU Member States. *Health Policy.* 2014; 118: 229–241. PMID: 252014533.

[121] Cruickshank C, Wise M, Schroder P. Pharmaceutical: Getting back its luster. A. T. Kearney. 2011. https://www.atkearney.com/health/ideas-insights/article/-/asset_publisher/LCcgOeS4t85g/content/pharmaceutical-getting-back-its-luster/10192. Accessed September 30, 2016.

[122] Gyurjan G, Parsons I, Thaker S. A health check for pharma: Overcoming change fatigue in the pharmaceutical industry. McKinsey & Company. 2014. http://www.mckinsey.com/industries/pharmaceuticals-and-medical-products/our-insights/a-health-check-for-pharma-overcoming-change-fatigue-in-the-pharmaceutical-industry. Accessed September 30, 2016.

[123] Basu P, et al. Analysis of manufacturing costs in pharmaceutical companies. *J Pharm Innov.* 2008; 3: 30–40. DOI: 10.1007/s12247-008-9024-4.

[124] SGEN Form 10-Q (Nov. 4, 2011).

[125] ACOR Form 10-K (2014).

[126] MDCO Form 10-K (2013).

[127] NovaBay expands sales force for Avenova. NBY press release. January 20, 2015. http://novabay.com/pressreleases/novabay-expands-sales-force-avenova/. Accessed September 30, 2016.

[128] Weinstein D. Human Genome Sciences spurns GSK's $3B offer. Medical Marketing & Media. April 19, 2012. http://www.mmm-online.com/channel/human-genome-sciences-spurns-gsks-3b-offer/article/237305/. Accessed September 30, 2016.

[129] HGS Form 10-K (2012).

[130] Waters W. Optimer to market Dificid drug with Cubist Pharmaceuticals. Bloomberg News. April 6, 2011. http://www.bloomberg.com/news/articles/2011-04-06/optimer-to-co-market-dificid-drug-with-cubist-pharmaceuticals. Accessed September 30, 2016.

[131] Serebrov M. Incyte scores big with the approval of first JAK inhibitor. BioWorld. http://www.bioworld.com/content/incyte-scores-big-approval-first-jak-inhibitor-0. Accessed September 30, 2016.

132 Orphan diseases: Rare rivalry. Medical Marketing & Media. April 1, 2013. http://www.mmm-online.com/features/orphan-diseases-rare-rivalry/article/286654/. Accessed September 30, 2016.

133 CHTP investor presentation. October 2011. http://www.sec.gov/Archives/edgar/data/1333763/000119312511274927/d245008dex991.htm. Accessed September 30, 2016.

134 Helfand C. Boehringer revs up Ofev sales force, support services to rival Roche's Esbriet in IPF. FiercePharma. October 21, 2014. http://www.fiercepharmamarketing.com/story/boehringer-revs-ofev-sales-force-support-services-rival-roches-esbriet-ipf/2014-10-21. Accessed September 30, 2016.

135 Staton T. Affymax approval breaks Amgen's long anemia monopoly. FiercePharma. March 28, 2012. http://www.fiercepharma.com/story/affymax-approval-breaks-amgens-long-anemia-monopoly/2012-03-28. Accessed September 30, 2016.

136 Theravance Biopharma, Inc. reports first quarter 2015 financial results. TBPH press release. May 7, 2015. http://investor.theravance.com/releasedetail.cfm?releaseid=911873. Accessed September 30, 2016.

137 Staton T. Xtandi field force gets a staffing boost for market-share battle with Zytiga. FiercePharma. September 15, 2014. http://www.fiercepharmamarketing.com/story/xtandi-field-force-gets-staffing-boost-market-share-battle-zytiga/2014-09-15. Accessed September 30, 2016. Number reflects combined sales force from both partners.

138 Wang T. Restructuring the pharmaceutical industry (industry focus, vol. 155). Mizuho Bank. May 2014. http://www.mizuhobank.com/fin_info/industry/index.html. Accessed September 30, 2016.

139 Armstrong D. Pfizer said to fire 20% of U.S. primary-care sales force. Bloomberg News. December 18, 2012. http://www.bloomberg.com/news/articles/2012-12-18/pfizer-to-fire-about-20-percent-of-u-s-primary-care-sales-force. Accessed September 30, 2016.

140 Staton T. Astellas presents The Bladder, animated pitch-organ for overactive-bladder med Myrbetriq. FiercePharma. March 26, 2014. http://www.fiercepharmamarketing.com/story/astellas-presents-bladder-animated-pitch-organ-overactive-bladder-med-myrbe/2014-03-26. Accessed September 30, 2016.

141 Edwards J. Death of a salesman: AstraZeneca replaced entire Nexium salesforce with telemarketers—and it worked. CBS Moneywatch. May 18, 2010. http://www.cbsnews.com/news/death-of-a-salesman-astrazeneca-replaced-entire-nexium-salesforce-with-telemarketers-and-it-worked/. Accessed September 30, 2016.

142 Iskowitz M. Pharma sales report: Special force. Medical Marketing & Media. November 1, 2011. http://www.mmm-online.com/features/pharma-sales-report-special-force/article/215171/. Accessed September 30, 2016.

143 Somaxon Pharmaceuticals, Inc. (SOMX), Procter & Gamble (PG) to launch insomnia drug in Sept., will co-promote Silenor with a combined 215 sales reps in the U.S. market, Somaxon stock rises at market close. BioSpace. August 25, 2010. http://www.biospace.com/news_story.aspx?StoryID=192063&full=1. Accessed September 30, 2016.

144 Timmerman L. Ironwood bucks the trends, makes big bet on drug for millions. Xconomy. February 6, 2013. http://www.xconomy.com/boston/2013/02/06/ironwood-bucks-the-trends-makes-big-bet-on-new-drug-for-millions/. Accessed September 30, 2016.

145 Horizon Pharma announces completion of sales force expansion. HZNP press release. October 1, 2012. http://ir.horizon-pharma.com/releasedetail.cfm?releaseid=710262. Accessed September 30, 2016.

146 Weinstein D. Takeda backs Contrave with 99 sales reps. Medical Marketing & Media. September 15, 2014. http://www.mmm-online.com/pharmaceutical/takeda-backs-contrave-with-900-sales-reps/article/371592/. Accessed September 30, 2016.

147 Staton T. Novo Nordisk puts 500 Saxenda reps on U.S. streets, aiming for $1B in weight-loss sales. FiercePharma. January 26, 2015. http://www.fiercepharma.com/story/novo-nordisk-puts-500-saxenda-reps-us-streets-aiming-1b-weight-loss-sales/2015-01-26. Accessed September 30, 2016.

148 Helfand C. Eisai rejig means sales-force downsizing at a critical moment for Arena's Belviq. FiercePharma. April 15, 2015. http://www.fiercepharma.com/marketing/eisai-rejig-means-sales-force-downsizing-at-a-critical-moment-for-arena-s-belviq. Accessed September 30, 2016.

149 Staton T. With Qsymia still flailing, Vivus to cut 20 jobs, replace CFO. FiercePharma. November 6, 2013. http://www.fiercepharma.com/story/qsymia-still-flailing-vivus-cut-20-jobs-replace-cfo/2013-11-06. Accessed September 30, 2016.

[150] Smart DR. *Physician Characteristics and Distribution in the U.S.*, 2012 edition. American Medical Association. 2012.

[151] Employer costs for employee compensation. Bureau of Labor Statistics. September 8, 2016. http://www.bls.gov/news.release/ecec.nr0.htm. Accessed September 30, 2016.

[152] Silverman E. The pharmaceutical sales rep lives to fight another day. *Wall Street Journal.* March 13, 2014. http://blogs.wsj.com/corporate-intelligence/2014/03/13/the-pharmaceutical-sales-rep-lives-to-fight-another-day/. Accessed September 30, 2016.

[153] 2016 medical sales salary report. MedReps. https://www.medreps.com/medical-sales-careers/medical-sales-salary-report/. Accessed September 30, 2016.

[154] ERI's national compensation forecast July 2016. Economic Research Institute. http://www.erieri.com/whitepapers. Accessed October 24, 2016.

[155] Employment cost trends. U.S. Bureau of Labor Statistics. http://www.bls.gov/ect/. Accessed October 24, 2016.

[156] Bolesh E. Launch on a budget. *Pharmaceutical Executive.* October 1, 2006. http://www.pharmexec.com/launch-budget. Accessed September 16, 2016.

[157] Kornfield R, et al. Promotion of prescription drugs to consumers and providers, 2001–2010. *PLOS One.* 2013; 8: e55504. PMID: 23469165.

[158] Kornfield R, et al. Promotion of prescription drugs to consumers and providers, 2001–2010. *PLOS One.* 2013; 8: e55504. PMID: 23469165.

[159] Dobrow L. A sunny day in Pharmaland: The 2015 pharma report. Medical Marketing & Media. April 27, 2015: 33–42. http://www.mmm-online.com/features/pharma-report-a-sunny-day-in-pharmaland/article/411060/. Accessed September 16, 2016.

[160] Dobrow L. How is pharma shifting its marketing budgets? Medical Marketing & Media. February 29, 2016. http://www.mmm-online.com/campaigns/how-is-pharma-shifting-its-marketing-budgets/article/478966/. Accessed September 16, 2016.

[161] Hughes JP, et al. Principles of early drug discovery. *Br J Pharmacol.* 2011; 162: 1239–1249. PMID: 21091654.

[162] Paul SM, et al. How to improve R&D productivity: the pharmaceutical industry's grand challenge. *Nat Rev Drug Disc.* 2010; 9:203–214. PMID: 20168317.

[163] Stergiopoulos S, Getz KA. Mapping and characterizing the development pathway from non-clinical through early clinical drug development. *Pharm Med.* 2012; 26:297–307. DOI: 10.1007/BF03262374.

[164] DiMasi JA, Grabowski HG, Hansen RW. Innovation in the pharmaceutical industry: New estimates of R&D costs. *J Health Econ.* 2016; 47: 20–33. DOI: 10.1007/BF03262374.

[165] Mestre-Ferrandiz J, Sussex J, Towse A. The R&D cost of a new medicine. Office of Health Economics. 2012. https://www.ohe.org/publications/rd-cost-new-medicine. Accessed September 28, 2016.

[166] Adams CP, Brantner VV. Estimating the cost of new drug development: Is it really $802 million? *Health Affairs.* 2006; 25: 420–428. PMID: 16522582.

[167] Paul SM, et al. How to improve R&D productivity: the pharmaceutical industry's grand challenge. *Nat Rev Drug Disc.* 2010; 9:203–214. PMID: 20168317.

[168] Mestre-Ferrandiz J, Sussex J, Towse A. The R&D cost of a new medicine. Office of Health Economics. 2012. https://www.ohe.org/publications/rd-cost-new-medicine. Accessed September 28, 2016.

[169] Orphan Drug Report 2015. EvaluatePharma. http://www.evaluategroup.com/public/reports/EvaluatePharma-Orphan-Drug-Report-2015.aspx. Accessed August 25, 2016.

[170] DiMasi JA, Grabowski HG, Hansen RW. Innovation in the pharmaceutical industry: New estimates of R&D costs. *J Health Econ.* 2016; 47: 20–33. DOI: 10.1007/BF03262374.

[171] Adams CP, Brantner VV. Estimating the cost of new drug development: Is it really $802 million? *Health Affairs.* 2006; 25: 420–428. PMID: 16522582.

[172] Pregelj L, Verreynne M-L, Hine D. Changes in clinical trial length. *Nat Rev Drug Disc.* 2015; 14: 307–308. PMID: 25924577.

[173] Adams CP, Brantner VV. Estimating the cost of new drug development: Is it really $802 million? *Health Affairs.* 2006; 25: 420–428. PMID: 16522582.

[174] Adams CP, Brantner VV. Estimating the cost of new drug development: Is it really $802 million? *Health Affairs.* 2006; 25: 420–428. PMID: 16522582.

[175] Kaitin KI, DiMasi JA. Pharmaceutical innovation in the 21st century: New drug approvals in the first decade, 2000–2009. *Clin Pharm Ther.* 2011; 89: 183–188. PMID: 21191382.

[176] DiMasi JA, Milne CP, Tabarrok A. An FDA report card: Wide variance in performance found among agency's drug review divisions. Manhattan Institute. 2014. https://www.manhattan-institute.org/html/fda-report-card-wide-variance -performance-found-among-agencys-drug-review-6015.html. Accessed August 25, 2016.

[177] Orphan Drug Report 2015. EvaluatePharma. http://www.evaluategroup.com/ public/reports/EvaluatePharma-Orphan-Drug-Report-2015.aspx. Accessed August 25, 2016.

[178] Kaitin KI, DiMasi JA. Pharmaceutical innovation in the 21st century: New drug approvals in the first decade, 2000–2009. *Clin Pharm Ther.* 2011; 89: 183–188. PMID: 21191382.

[179] Shea M, et al. Impact of breakthrough designation on cancer drug development. *Nat Rev Drug Disc.* 2016; 15: 152. PMID: 26931085.

[180] Sertkaya A, et al. Examination of clinical trial costs and barriers for drug development. Eastern Research Group, Inc. 2014. https://aspe.hhs.gov/report/ examination-clinical-trial-costs-and-barriers-drug-development. Accessed September 6, 2016.

[181] Belleli R, Fisch R. Efficiency indicators for new drugs approved by the FDA from 2003 to 2013. *Nat Rev Drug Disc.* 2015; 14: 156. PMID: 25722232.

[182] Orphan Drug Report 2015. EvaluatePharma. http://www.evaluategroup.com/ public/reports/EvaluatePharma-Orphan-Drug-Report-2015.aspx. Accessed August 25, 2016.

[183] Measures of clinical trial costs, 2011–2012. In: *Parexel Biopharmaceutical R&D Statistical Sourcebook 2013/2014.* Waltham, MA: Parexel International Corporation; 2013: 165.

[184] Biopharmaceutical industry-sponsored clinical trials: Impact on state economies. PhRMA. March 2015. http://catalyst.phrma.org/new-report-clinical-trials-and-the -impact-on-state-economies. Accessed September 6, 2016.

[185] DiMasi JA, Grabowski HG, Hansen RW. Innovation in the pharmaceutical industry: New estimates of R&D costs. *J Health Econ.* 2016; 47: 20–33. DOI: 10.1007/BF03262374.

[186] Paul SM, et al. How to improve R&D productivity: the pharmaceutical industry's grand challenge. *Nat Rev Drug Disc.* 2010; 9:203–214. PMID: 20168317.

[187] Mestre-Ferrandiz J, Sussex J, Towse A. The R&D cost of a new medicine. Office of Health Economics. 2012. https://www.ohe.org/publications/rd-cost-new-medicine. Accessed September 28, 2016.

[188] Orphan Drug Report 2015. EvaluatePharma. http://www.evaluategroup.com/public/reports/EvaluatePharma-Orphan-Drug-Report-2015.aspx. Accessed August 25, 2016.

[189] Sertkaya A, et al. Examination of clinical trial costs and barriers for drug development. Eastern Research Group, Inc. 2014. https://aspe.hhs.gov/report/examination-clinical-trial-costs-and-barriers-drug-development. Accessed September 6, 2016.

[190] CADX Form 10-K (2012).

[191] NBY Form 10-K (2015).

[192] VVUS Form 10-K (2015).

[193] Thomas DW, et al. Clinical development success rates, 2006–2015. Biotechnology Innovation Organization. https://www.bio.org/bio-industry-analysis-published-reports. Accessed September 1, 2016.

[194] Downing NS, et al. Characterizing the US FDA's approach to promoting transformative innovation. *Nat Rev Drug Disc.* 2015; 14: 740–741. PMID: 26435528.

[195] Belleli R, Fisch R. Efficiency indicators for new drugs approved by the FDA from 2003 to 2013. *Nat Rev Drug Disc.* 2015; 14: 156. PMID: 25722232.

[196] Schick A, et al. What drives differences in review times among CDER divisions? *Nat Rev Drug Disc.* 2015; 14: 670–671. PMID: 26294264.

[197] DiMasi JA, Milne CP, Tabarrok A. An FDA report card: Wide variance in performance found among agency's drug review divisions. Manhattan Institute. 2014. https://www.manhattan-institute.org/html/fda-report-card-wide-variance-performance-found-among-agencys-drug-review-6015.html. Accessed August 25, 2016.

[198] Orphan Drug Report 2015. EvaluatePharma. http://www.evaluategroup.com/ public/reports/EvaluatePharma-Orphan-Drug-Report-2015.aspx. Accessed August 25, 2016.

[199] DiMasi JA, Grabowski HG, Hansen RW. Innovation in the pharmaceutical industry: New estimates of R&D costs. *J Health Econ.* 2016; 47: 20–33. DOI: 10.1007/BF03262374.

[200] Paul SM, et al. How to improve R&D productivity: the pharmaceutical industry's grand challenge. *Nat Rev Drug Disc.* 2010; 9:203–214. PMID: 20168317.

[201] Prescription drug user fee rates for fiscal year 2017. U.S. Food and Drug Administration. 81 FR 49674. July 28, 2016. https://www.federalregister.gov/ articles/2016/07/28/2016-17870/prescription-drug-user-fee-rates-for-fiscal -year-2017. Accessed August 31, 2016.

[202] Fees payable to the European Medicines Agency. European Medicines Agency. http://www.ema.europa.eu/ema/index.jsp?curl=pages/regulation/document_listing/ document_listing_000327.jsp. Accessed August 31, 2016.

[203] Japan Drug Regulatory Overview 2014. Pacific Bridge Medical. http://www.pacificbridgemedical.com/wp-content/uploads/2015/04/Japan-Drug -Regulatory-Overview-2014.pdf. Accessed August 31, 2016.

[204] DiMasi JA, et al. Trends in risks associated with new drug development: Success rates for investigational drugs. *Clin Pharm Ther.* 2010; 87: 272–277. PMID: 20130567.

[205] Paul SM, et al. How to improve R&D productivity: the pharmaceutical industry's grand challenge. *Nat Rev Drug Disc.* 2010; 9:203–214. PMID: 20168317.

[206] Hay M, et al. Clinical development success rates for investigational drugs. *Nat Biotech.* 2014; 32: 40–51.

[207] Smietana K, et al. Improving R&D productivity. *Nat Rev Drug Disc.* 2015; 14: 455–456. PMID: 24406927.

[208] DiMasi JA, Grabowski HG, Hansen RW. Innovation in the pharmaceutical industry: New estimates of R&D costs. *J Health Econ.* 2016; 47: 20–33. DOI: 10.1007/BF03262374.

[209] Smietana K, Siatkowski M, Moller M. Trends in clinical success rates. *Nat Rev Drug Disc.* 2016; 15: 379–380. PMID: 27199245.

210 Thomas DW, et al. Clinical development success rates, 2006–2015. Biotechnology Innovation Organization. https://www.bio.org/bio-industry-analysis -published-reports. Accessed September 1, 2016.

211 Hughes JP, et al. Principles of early drug discovery. *Br J Pharmacol.* 2011; 162: 1239–1249. PMID: 21091654.

212 Waring MJ, et al. An analysis of the attrition of drug candidates from four major pharmaceutical companies. *Nat Rev Drug Disc.* 2015; 14: 475–486. PMID: 26091267.

213 Cummings JL, Morstorf T, Zhong K. Alzheimer's disease drug-development pipeline: few candidates, frequent failures. *Alz Res Therapy.* 2014; 6: 37. PMID: 25024750.

214 Success rates in clinical development: large vs. small molecule rates. KMR Group. September 15, 2015. https://kmrgroup.com/in-the-news/. Accessed November 9, 2016.

215 Success rates in clinical development: large vs. small molecule rates. KMR Group. September 15, 2015. https://kmrgroup.com/in-the-news/. Accessed November 9, 2016.

216 Gallo A. A refresher on cost of capital. *Harvard Business Review.* April 30, 2015. https://hbr.org/2015/04/a-refresher-on-cost-of-capital. Accessed August 16, 2016.

217 NPV vs. rNPV. Avance. February 2011. www.avance.ch/newsletter/docs/avance_ on_NPV_vs_rNPV.pdf. Accessed August 16, 2016.

218 Drug development: Valuing the pipeline—a UK study. Mayer Brown. March 2009. https://www.mayerbrown.com/publications/. Accessed August 16, 2016.

219 Discount rates for biotech companies. Avance. January 2008. www.avance.ch/ newsletter/docs/discount_1.pdf. Accessed August 16, 2016.

220 Baras AI, Baras AS, Schulman KA. Drug development risk and the cost of capital. *Nat Rev Drug Disc.* 2012; 11: 347–348. PMID: 22498751.

221 Villiger R, Nielsen NH. Discount rates in drug development. January 2011. www.avance.ch/avance_biostrat_discount_survey.pdf. Accessed August 16, 2016.

222 Baras AI, Baras AS, Schulman KA. Drug development risk and the cost of capital. *Nat Rev Drug Disc.* 2012; 11: 347–348. PMID: 22498751.

[223] David E, Tramontin T, Zemmel R. The road to positive R&D returns. McKinsey & Company. February 2010. http://www.mckinsey.com/industries/pharmaceuticals -and-medical-products/our-insights/the-road-to-positive-r-and-38d-returns. Accessed August 16, 2016.

[224] Measuring the return from pharmaceutical innovation 2015. Deloitte Centre for Health Solutions. http://www2.deloitte.com/uk/en/pages/life-sciences-and -healthcare/articles/measuring-return-from-pharmaceutical-innovation.html. Accessed August 16, 2016.

ABOUT THE AUTHORS

 **FRANK S. DAVID, MD, PHD,** is a corporate strategist and physician-scientist working at the intersection of business, clinical medicine, and basic research. He is the founder and managing director of Pharmagellan, a healthcare consulting firm that helps established and emerging biomedical companies, entrepreneurs, and investors unlock the financial and strategic value of innovative R&D.

Before founding Pharmagellan in 2013, Frank was director of strategy in AstraZeneca's Oncology Innovative Medicines unit, where he focused on programs from target identification through Phase 2a clinical studies. He spearheaded initiatives in end-to-end franchise strategy and portfolio valuation, led external communications aimed at R&D collaborators and investors, and provided commercial support to pipeline projects and in-licensing teams.

Before working at AstraZeneca, Frank was a director in the consulting arm of Leerink Partners, where he led advisory engagements for corporate, commercial, R&D, business development, and investor clients across all major therapeutic areas and healthcare business sectors, including biotech, pharma, devices, diagnostics, life sciences tools, and healthcare services. He cofounded Leerink's Transactional Consulting practice, which advised financial and strategic investors and early-stage companies side by side with Leerink's investment banking team.

In addition to his work with Pharmagellan, Frank is an innovation strategist at the Brigham Research Institute of Brigham and Women's Hospital, and an active mentor of early-stage healthcare companies and entrepreneurs in MassBio's MassCONNECT program. Frank's work in healthcare strategy and related topics has been published in *Nature Reviews Drug Discovery, In Vivo, Pharmaceutical Executive,* and *Mayo Clinic Proceedings.* He also blogs about biomedical innovation at Forbes.com, and is active on Twitter (@Frank_S_David).

Frank earned his BS from Yale University in molecular biophysics and biochemistry, and his MD and PhD from Columbia University and its College of Physicians and Surgeons. A board-certified pathologist, he completed his clinical and postdoctoral research training at Brigham and Women's Hospital, then joined the faculty of Harvard Medical School and Brigham and Women's, where he led an NIH-funded basic research group focused on cell signaling in cancer and kidney development.

SETH ROBEY, PHD, was an associate consultant at Pharmagellan from 2014 to 2016. Before joining Pharmagellan, Seth explored key issues in clinical development, regulatory affairs, and biopharma equity analysis as a freelance contributor to the Motley Fool, where he regularly wrote articles reviewing market-moving developments in healthcare. After completing his tenure at Pharmagellan, Seth earned his PhD in pharmacology and molecular signaling from Columbia University, and joined Merck's Quantitative Pharmacology and Pharmacometrics group as a senior scientist.

ANDREW MATTHEWS, MD, has been an associate consultant at Pharmagellan since 2014. He received his MD at Thomas Jefferson University and is continuing his clinical training in internal medicine at Harvard's Beth Israel Deaconess Medical Center. Before medical school, he was an associate in Leerink Swann's healthcare strategy consulting practice, where he focused on life cycle management, asset scans, and valuation. Andy earned his BA in biology at the University of Pennsylvania and his BS in economics from Penn's Wharton School.

Made in the USA
Middletown, DE
25 November 2019

79446623R00083